5 INGREDIENT
COOKBOOK

*QUICK & EASY RECIPES TO MAKE
HEALTHY EATING SIMPLE*

BY FINLEY MACK

© **Copyright 2022 by – Finley Mack - All rights reserved.**

This document is geared towards providing exact and reliable information in regards to the topic and issue covered. The publication is sold with the idea that the publisher is not required to render accounting, officially permitted, or otherwise, qualified services. If advice is necessary, legal or professional, a practiced individual in the profession should be ordered.

- From a Declaration of Principles which was accepted and approved equally by a Committee of the American Bar Association and a Committee of Publishers and Associations.

In no way is it legal to reproduce, duplicate, or transmit any part of this document in either electronic means or in printed format. Recording of this publication is strictly prohibited and any storage of this document is not allowed unless with written permission from the publisher. All rights reserved.

The information provided herein is stated to be truthful and consistent, in that any liability, in terms of inattention or otherwise, by any usage or abuse of any policies, processes, or directions contained within is the solitary and utter responsibility of the recipient reader. Under no reparation, damages, or monetary loss due to the information herein, either directly or indirectly.

All data and information provided in this book is for informational purposes only. Finley Mack makes no representations as to accuracy, completeness, current, suitability, or validity of any information in this book & will not be liable for any errors, omissions, or delays in this information or any losses, injuries, or damages arising from its display or use. All information is provided on an as-is basis. Respective authors own all copyrights not held by the publisher.

The information herein is offered for informational purposes solely, and is universal as so. The presentation of the information is without contract or any type of guarantee assurance.

The trademarks that are used are without any consent, and the publication of the trademark is without permission or backing by the trademark owner. All trademarks and brands within this book are for clarifying purposes only and are owned by the owners themselves, not affiliated with this document.

The author is not a licensed practitioner, physician or medical professional and offers no medical treatment, diagnoses, suggestions or counselling. The information presented herein has not been evaluated by the U.S Food & Drug Administration, and it is not intended to diagnose, treat, cure or prevent any disease. Full medical clearance from a licensed physician should be obtained before beginning or modifying any diet, exercise or lifestyle program, and physician should be informed of all nutritional changes. The author claims no responsibility to any person or entity for any liability, loss, damage or death caused or alleged to be caused directly or indirectly as a result of the use, application or interpretation of the information presented herein.

TABLE OF CONTENTS

INTRODUCTION..........................5
  Why 5 Ingredients?............................ 7
  Save Time at the Grocery Store................. 7
  Ingredients to Always Have in Your Pantry 8
  Focus on Flexible Flavor 10
  5 Tips for 5-Ingredient Meals 11
  Cooking Is No Longer a Chore.................12

BREAKFASTS 13
  Everyday Parfait 14
  Egg-in-the-Basket Sandwich 15
  Bodybuilder's Muffins 16
  Ham-and-Cheese Breakfast Baguette 17
  Lazy Sunday Mini-Quiches 18
  Breakfast Hash Pies 19
  Turkey Meatball and Vegetable Hash 20
  Quinoa, Oatmeal-Style........................21
  Citrusy French Toast 22
  Easy Homemade Donuts........................23
  Cheesy Homemade Muffins 24
  Banana Flapjacks 25
  Chicken Sandwiches for Brunch 26
  No-Carb Ham-and-Hollandaise Cups...........27
  Egg-and-Bacon Tacos 28

SNACKS AND HORS D'OEUVRES 29
  Spiral Pizzas 30
  Sweet Potato and Blue Cheese Poutine.........31
  Simple Hummus..............................32
  California Crab Puffs 33
  Miniature Baguettes with Honey-and-Chili Dip...34
  Braised Pork Nachos 35
  Cheesy Sticks 36
  Asian Chicken Tartlets.......................37
  Caramel Apple and Brie Kabobs...............38
  Cheesy Broccoli Dip..........................39

  Diet-Busting Choco-Coco Balls 40
  Greek Pizzettas..............................41
  Poor Man's Chocolate Eclairs 42
  Hot Olive Dip................................43

POULTRY 44
  Thanksgiving Monday Dinner..................45
  Low-Carb Chicken Enchiladas 46
  Turkey Breast with Honey-Mustard Glaze 47
  Basil Chicken Spaghetti 48
  Country-Style Chicken Pie....................49
  Individual Chicken Calzones 50
  Citrus Chicken with Asparagus 51
  Chicken with Herby Quinoa 52
  Garlicky Chicken Sandwiches 53
  Faux-BBQ Chicken 54
  Chicken Skewers.............................55
  Savory Waffles with Chicken 56
  Fragrant Chicken with Cauliflower Rice 57
  Roast Chicken with Spiced Yogurt 58

SEAFOOD & FISH.....................59
  Peppery Salmon Fillets with String Beans......60
  Steamed Salmon with Buttery Asparagus 61
  Pan-Fried Teriyaki Fish 62
  Breaded Flounder............................63
  Poisson en Papillote with Roast Potatoes 64
  Japanese-Style Sea Bass 65
  Sriracha Shrimp Patties......................66
  Saucy Seafood Tacos 67
  Easy Oven-Baked Salmon 68
  Broiled Lobster Tails 69
  Fish with Latin-Style Rice 70
  Italian Rice with Shrimp 71
  Salmon Fishcakes 72

BEEF, LAMB & PORK 73

- Hawaiian Beef Wraps 74
- BBQ Pulled Beef Sandwiches 75
- One-Pan Beef Dinner 76
- Peppers Stuffed with Rice and Beef 77
- Fried Rice with Kimchi 78
- Pork Chops with Tangy String Beans 79
- Grilled Indian Adana Kabobs 80
- Mediterranean Lamb Chops 81
- Corned Beef Calzones 82
- Cheesy Beef Burritos 83
- Braised Beef with Cranberry Gravy 84
- Toasted Tortillas with Beans 85
- Slightly Spicy Roast Pork 86
- Breaded Pork Cutlets with Herbs 87

COMFORT FOOD 88

- Crazy Weekday Beef-and-Pasta Soup 89
- Feel-Good Sliders 90
- Wisconsin Beer Brats 91
- (Nearly) Instant Gumbo 92
- Creamy Shrimp and Broccoli Pasta 93
- Kebab Meat in Pita Pockets 94
- Stir-Fried Black Bean Sauce Chicken 95
- Strip Steaks with Sauteed Potatoes 96
- Kale and Mushroom Tagliatelle 97
- Roman Carbonara 98
- Chewy Meat Calzone 99
- Asian Beef Noodles 100
- Simple Cowherd's Pie 101

VEGETARIAN MAIN COURSES 102

- Zucchini Casserole 103
- Super-Simple Broccoli Soup 104
- Autumn Soup 105
- Spaghetti Squash Vegan "Bolognese" 106
- Fusilli with Tomato and Spinach 107
- Upgraded Vegetarian Enchilada 108
- Sun-Dried Tomato Gnocchi 109
- Soba Noodles with Japanese Spices and Asparagus 110
- Cauliflower and Cheese Casserole 111
- Back-to-Basics Pizza 112
- Black Bean Quesadillas with Sweet Potato Mash . 113
- Spiced Red Lentils with Crispy Shallots 114
- Fried Rice with Chinese Cabbage 115
- Ravioli in Browned Butter Sauce 116
- Farm-Style Butternut Squash Tart 117

SALADS & SIDE DISHES 118

- Easy Potatoes au Gratin 119
- Caprese Salad 119
- Popeye Salad 120
- Spanish Rice 120
- Carrots Sauteed with Ginger 121
- Fruity Black Beans 121
- Asian Sauteed Zucchini 122
- Warm Quinoa and Brussels Sprouts Salad 122
- Italian Green Beans 123

DESSERTS 124

- Imitation Hazelnut Pie 125
- Oven-Baked S'mores 126
- Vanilla-and-Fruit Kolaches 127
- White Chocolate Rice Krispies Treats 128
- Easy Blueberry Cobbler 129
- Vanilla Cake with Cookie Pieces 130
- Almond Biscottis 131
- Seasonal Berry Blanc Mange 132
- Baklava Made Easy 133
- Toasted Angel Food Cake 134
- Nutty Chocolate Squares 135
- Homemade Chocolate Truffles 136
- Pear Pie 137

INTRODUCTION

Do you groan every night when you have to think of something to cook the family for dinner? It seems like such a thankless task that comes around every 24 hours. And of course there's also breakfast, lunch, and snacks to think about. Why do people need to eat? If only there was a way to make cooking easier, cheaper, and more time efficient.

When you page through a recipe book or scroll through mouth-watering recipes online, you might feel inspired to treat your family to a meal that blows their socks off. But then you look at the list of ingredients and it's longer than your arm! You only have a handful of them in the pantry and you don't have time to go out and do yet another round of grocery shopping. So, you put the book away or shut down your phone's browser and resort to cooking the same old thing you cook every week.

I feel your pain! I love cooking. I particularly enjoy trying new recipes. But when said recipes ask for ingredients that I don't normally keep in my pantry, I tend to move on to the next one rather quickly. Next thing I know, I am feeling frustrated, and because I have a hungry husband and son breathing down my neck, wanting to know what's for dinner, I make something that I know is quick and easy, even though we eat it all…the…time.

What I have found, though, is that with a little bit of creativity, I can create a meal from very little that everyone enjoys. My husband often goes into the kitchen with the best of intentions, looking for something to cook, and comes back to me to say that there is nothing in the fridge. And then he wonders how I came up with an amazing meal from the pantry's meager contents!

Sometimes I will serve my family the most basic meal – like a grilled steak with baked potatoes and frozen vegetables. But some of the best meals come from using a collection of leftover ingredients that I bought for a fancy meal when we had people around for dinner over the weekend. When you combine something a little more special with your more everyday food, the result is often spectacular.

That's where the 5-ingredient recipes come from that are presented in this book – it's an attempt at adding a little something special to meals that you cook all the time because they are quick and easy. In this way, this collection of recipes is different. When you page through the recipes that I have carefully put together for you, not only will you feel inspired, but you will be able to prepare them without making a special trip to the grocery store and spending a small fortune!

Also, these recipes are not exclusively for families. They are perfect for someone living on their own who has to cook for themselves every day, which can be a real chore. Takeout is so much easier! These recipes are also great for new couples who haven't had to cook on a regular basis before leaving the family nest.

Using only 5 ingredients means you get to save some money. When you shop smart, you will have all the necessary food items stocked in your pantry, just waiting for you to create your next delicious, time-efficient, and economical meal. No one will know that you used a neat little foodie trick here and there to deliver on your promise of having a tasty meal on the table by 7pm every night.

WHY 5 INGREDIENTS?

To answer a question with a question: Why make life more complicated than it needs to be? Even famous chefs cook amazing meals with just 5 ingredients. In my opinion, the simpler the food, the better it tastes.

We live in a world that has us rushing from one thing to the next. Monday runs into Tuesday, which runs into Wednesday, and before you know it, you have raced through the weekend and you're starting again on Monday. With so many commitments, who has time to cook? More importantly, who has time to cook anything that requires taking 20 different grocery items out of the cupboard and painstakingly measuring them, chopping them, or sautéing them so as to create a dinner that no one has time to fully appreciate?

So, I've taken the fuss out of everyday cooking and created a collection of recipes that you can whip up in a jiffy. Even getting the ingredients ready is quick and easy. There obviously has to be some preparation involved, otherwise you might as well just shop in the frozen food section, but if you only have to take out, measure, and prepare 5 ingredients, you can be done with the preparation in 5 minutes. Then all that's left to do is get on with cooking your dinner.

SAVE TIME AT THE GROCERY STORE

Almost as bad as spending hours in the kitchen is the weekly trip to the grocery store. Grocery stores are filled with shopping trolleys that have squeaky, wobbly wheels that don't ever seem to go where you steer them and other shoppers who are just as frustrated as you are about having to take precious time out of their day to buy food or ingredients to make food for their families every…single…day. And that's not even to mention the huge array of products from which to choose.

The experience of shopping can be seriously overwhelming at the best of times, but then someone asks you to quickly pop into the shop on your way home. Or you have decided to cook something that needs an ingredient that you don't have. So, you find yourself back among the aisles of food and trolleys and people on a day that you normally wouldn't go to the store.

Wouldn't it be better to shop smarter so you could cut down on grocery shopping? I'm guessing that you try. I try too, but I don't always get it right. Life has a way of changing direction at the last minute. Forgetting an essential ingredient when doing your major grocery shop for the month might not seem like a big deal, but it can be a deal breaker – the difference between having a happy mother at the dinner table, or a grumpy one. It can mean warming up a frozen dinner instead of preparing something fresh and healthy.

Here are my 5 tips for making grocery shopping quicker, easier, and less expensive:

1. **Start with fresh ingredients.** The foods that give you the most bang for your buck are the fresh ones. They are full of natural, healthy flavor, and if you buy fresh produce such as fruit and vegetables that are in season, you will save some money too.

2. **Your freezer is your best friend.** Your freezer is not just for storing meat, fish, and chicken. Frozen vegetables come already prepared – all you have to do is cook them. Frozen berries and other fruit are handy to have on hand – they can be used in a variety of ways. You can also use your freezer to store already cooked rice, pasta sauces, and beans – all you have to do is cook a little extra when already preparing a meal. If you have leftover rotisserie chicken, for example, freeze it – you can use it to make pasta or burritos or a quick chicken and broccoli bake.

3. **Add flavor with commercial products.** While fresh sauces usually taste better than ones that come out of a jar, don't be afraid to experiment with commercial products that have the flavor already developed and ready to use. Think canned soups, ready-made pestos, canned tomatoes with garlic and herbs, packaged rice mixes, rubs, and seasoning blends. You have enough on your plate (excuse the pun!), you don't have to spend hours in the kitchen developing fabulous flavors.

4. **Use prepared food as a starting point for your meal.** Rotisserie chicken; prepared salads; and washed, peeled, and chopped vegetables all have their place in your kitchen. Half of the problem with the chore of daily cooking is the amount of time it takes to get the food ready to cook. Save the preparation involved in lengthy recipes for those days when you can and want to spend a little more time in the kitchen.

5. **Make a list.** Everyone tells you to make a shopping list before you head out. Why? Because it's the best way to make sure you don't have to make a second or third trip to the store. It is also the best way to make sure your pantry is stocked with all of the ingredients you use most often (i.e., the things that form the basis of your daily family meals).

INGREDIENTS TO ALWAYS HAVE IN YOUR PANTRY

When I say 5 ingredients in this book, I generally mean literally 5 ingredients. But, there are certain extra things that I assume you'll already have in the cupboard or fridge as standard that you will need from time to time. The absolute basics like water, salt, pepper, and oil are so common that they don't really count towards your ingredients list. Also, if I suggest something that might add a little zing to a meal but which isn't absolutely necessary, you may find it takes the full list of ingredients over 5.

I'm sure you'll agree, though, that a little leeway is a good thing, especially in the kitchen. Imagine making a lemon-honey chicken dish and the sixth and final ingredient was lemon juice but you choose to leave it out because the ingredients list wasn't under 5! The dish would be terribly disappointing.

Aside from the number 5, here is a list of ingredients that I think you should always have on hand. If you have a well-stocked pantry, you will always be able to whip something up, even at a moment's notice.

In the pantry:

- Salt
- Pepper
- A variety of dried herbs (e.g., rosemary, basil, oregano, thyme)
- A variety of dried spices (e.g., cumin, cinnamon, turmeric, paprika)
- Flour – all-purpose flour and corn flour
- Broth

- Oil
- Vinegars (e.g., red wine, apple cider, balsamic)
- Canned or condensed soup (e.g., chicken, mushroom, tomato)
- Salsa
- Pasta (e.g., macaroni, spaghetti, fettuccine)
- Tomato paste
- Tomato sauce
- Canned tomatoes, especially diced ones
- A variety of canned beans, lentils, and chickpeas
- Bread
- Rice
- Honey
- Hot sauce
- Breadcrumbs
- Mustard
- Soy sauce
- Couscous

Fresh ingredients:

- Lemons
- Garlic
- Onions
- Potatoes
- Tomatoes
- Carrots
- Spinach

In the fridge and freezer:

- Eggs
- Butter
- Milk
- Cheese
- Frozen vegetables (e.g., mixed vegetables, peas, spinach)
- Salad dressings
- Bacon

FOCUS ON FLEXIBLE FLAVOR

don't expect anyone to eat bland, boring food. You may be wondering where the flavor comes from if you are only using 5 ingredients in your meals. After all, don't awesome taste sensations come from layering aromatic ingredients and cooking them to develop their flavor? That may be true in some cases, such as a good curry, but modern cooking means that we don't have to rely on lots of single ingredients to create a smashing meal.

If you are a purist, you are probably squirming in your seat with smoke coming out of your ears by now. I hear you. I feel the same way – most of the time. But occasionally even the best cooks fall back on convenient ingredients. Isn't it better to use something someone else has taken the time to prepare if it helps you get dinner on the table without too much of a time commitment?

I was chatting to a friend about how her husband loves a good curry, but, like so many mothers, she is run off her feet and can't bear the thought of spending hours developing the intricate flavors that you find in a good curry after making sure everyone has been where they needed to go and done their homework. She told me that in order to make her life easier when making curry, she uses a cook-in sauce that she keeps in her pantry. It means that everyone can enjoy the food they love while mom doesn't have to do much more than fry some onion and chicken.

I must admit that I, too, have taken to keeping such sauces that simply have to be added to the pan on hand in order to put a tasty meal on the table. It's not cheating. It's recognizing that there are other things that have to be done and we only have 24 hours in a day. With that said, consider keeping some of these flavor sensations in your pantry:

- Cook-in curry sauce
- Jarred pasta sauce (Note: you don't have to use these sauces only in pasta; they make a great quick and easy addition to a number of meals)
- Curry pastes
- BBQ sauce
- Olives
- Mixed spices
- Sriracha sauce
- Capers
- Chutney
- Tapenade
- Marinated bell peppers
- Marinades
- Pestos

5 TIPS FOR 5-INGREDIENT MEALS

Everyday meals don't need to be complicated. In fact, unless you love cooking and have the time to spend in the kitchen every day cooking up amazing meals from long lists of ingredients, the cooking you do on a daily basis should be as simple as possible. That doesn't mean you have to compromise on flavor. If you are clever about the types of ingredients you keep in your fridge and pantry, you are all set to make every mealtime amazing – and you won't need rely on the frozen convenience meals at the grocery store!

Here are my top 5 tips for cooking 5-ingredient meals:

1. **Start with the flavor.** If you have some leftover pesto in the fridge, think about what you could add it to so as to make a mouth-watering dish. I have used pesto to make pasta dishes, fish cakes, and even chickpea patties. It is also great on homemade pizza! Similarly, if you have some sun-dried tomatoes handy, they could be the flavor bomb for a quick all-in-one chicken and rice dish, or you could blend them into some cream cheese for a quick pasta sauce. Remember to also use the flavor combinations that someone else has prepared, as this will mean that you only have to buy one package instead of fifteen different ingredients.

2. **Use ready mixes in different ways.** Who says you have to only make muffins from a muffin mix, or pancakes from a pancake mix? There are many different ways that these types of ingredients can be used. You could make cookies, bars, or batter for fritters, depending on what you're making. Noodles can be used for stir-fries, or crushed and sprinkled over salads to add an interesting crunch. Salsa can be added to a rice dish or pasta sauce, or used as a topping for baked fish. Be creative and think outside the box.

3. **Add your own interesting ingredients to basic ready-made food.** Rotisserie chicken, stuffing, and precooked rice are just three examples of foods that you can dress up in no time at all. You can eat the chicken as a meal on its own with the usual sides, or you could shred it and serve it on wraps. Alternatively, you could cut the chicken into pieces, cover it in a creamy tomato soup, and serve it on rice with a side of frozen vegetables. Some things are great as they are, but you can also make them your own by adding a few simple ingredients.

4. **Let simple ingredients hold the spotlight.** Don't be shy to keep it simple. Some of the best meals let only a handful of ingredients do all the talking. Traditional Italian pasta dishes, for example, are usually made from just a few fresh ingredients that are full of flavor. And, nothing beats a perfectly grilled steak with a splash of garlic butter served with a fluffy baked potato.

5. **Make it up as you go along.** Okay, I know not everyone has the confidence to play around in the kitchen, but it's something I absolutely love to do. It does mean that I often don't know how to replicate what I've created, however, bit it always turns out great! You also don't have to go big and create your own recipes from scratch. But, if you find that you are missing one of the five ingredients listed in one of this book's recipes, why not think about what would be a suitable substitute? You may just end up creating a new, magnificent dish that your family will enjoy for years to come.

COOKING IS NO LONGER A CHORE

There is no need to feel like you have to drag yourself into the kitchen at the end of yet another long, busy day. 5-ingredient meals are the answer to eating fabulous meals even when all you have is 20 minutes to whip up dinner for a hungry family.

Whether you are cooking for a family of four, just for you and your partner, or even just for yourself, 5-ingredient recipes take the work out of your daily meals. They are quick and easy to prepare, and best of all, there is very little measuring and chopping needed before the food even makes it to the stove. These recipes are a way to help you save both time and money, because you don't have to buy long lists of ingredients every time you want to make a delicious meal.

And, even when you are only using 5 ingredients, you can still let your creativity loose. Having some clever tricks up your sleeve can mean that you will look like a foodie genius. Simply keep your pantry stocked with the items you use most often, and make sure to keep some sensational taste ingredients handy too. Turn the convenience of modern food ingredients like sauces, canned tomatoes, and curry pastes into dishes that you can proudly call your own.

Are you ready to dive into this collection of 5-ingredient recipes that will surprise you and your friends and family with their wonderful aromas and tastes? Then let's get going – these recipes will make your life simpler and more delicious, all with just 5 ingredients!

BREAKFASTS

BREAKFASTS

EVERYDAY PARFAIT

An elegant breakfast doesn't have to take long to prepare...
nor do you even have to turn on the stove.

PREP TIME: 15 MINS | SERVINGS: 4

Ingredients:

- 4 cups plain low-fat yogurt
- 1 drop vanilla essence
- 2 peaches, chopped
- 2 cups mixed berries
- ½ cup granola

Directions:

1. Stir or beat the vanilla essence into the yogurt.
2. Starting with either kind of fruit, spoon layers (½- to 1") thick into mason jars or similar containers.
3. Alternate yogurt, granola, and fruits to create an attractive look.
4. You can serve these treats fresh, or keep them in the refrigerator for up to 24 hours.

Tips:
- Nearly any combination of fruit will work with this dish.
- Made the night before, this makes for a great on-the-go breakfast. You can also serve it in sundae glasses for an easy, nutritious dessert.

BREAKFASTS

EGG-IN-THE-BASKET SANDWICH

A tasty, high-protein breakfast can set you up for the rest of the day – both mentally and physically.

COOKING TIME: 15 MINS | SERVINGS: 1

Ingredients:

- 2 strips bacon
- 2 slices artisanal bread
- Mayonnaise to taste
- 1 egg
- 1 slice cheese – cheddar, pepper jack, or Swiss

Directions:

1. Place the bacon in a large, non-stick pan with a lid. Fry until crispy.

2. While the bacon is frying, use a cookie cutter of about 2" in diameter to make a hole in the middle of one slice of bread.

3. Cover one side of each slice of bread with mayonnaise.

4. Set the fried bacon aside and add the bread slice with a hole in it to the pan – mayonnaise-side down.

5. Flip the bread after 2-3 minutes and then break an egg into the hole. Lay down the other, whole slice of bread to toast next to it, mayonnaise-side down. Place the cheese and bacon on top of this slice to heat.

6. Put the lid on the pan and leave for about 3 minutes on moderate heat. Once the cheese has melted slightly and the yolk is no longer runny, you can flip the bread slice holding the egg onto the cheese and bacon. Enjoy your hearty breakfast sandwich!

Tip: Using mayonnaise instead of butter isn't just because it's easier to spread; the outside of your sandwich will end up much crispier this way.

BREAKFASTS

LAZY SUNDAY MINI-QUICHES

This unpretentious dish more than rewards the tiny amount of effort needed to prepare it.

COOKING TIME: 20 MINS | SERVINGS: 2

Ingredients:

- 4 strips of bacon
- 4 eggs
- 1/3 cup light cream
- ½ cup cheese, grated
- 2 scallions, chopped

Directions:

1. Pre-heat the oven to 350 °F (180 °C).

2. Fry the bacon until the fat starts to melt out of it, but remove the pan from the heat before it starts to get crispy. Place each rasher on a paper towel to remove excess grease.

3. While the bacon is cooking, beat 2 of the eggs together with the cream. Add alt and pepper to taste.

4. Prepare two small (cup-sized) baking dishes (or use two hollows of a muffin tin with large molds) with cooking spray and then line the outside with two strips of bacon each. Then add some cheese and scallions.

5. Pour half the egg mixture into each mold and add a whole egg on top. Garnish with a little bit of cheese and chopped scallions.

6. Bake for around 20 minutes – the breakfast is ready once the yolks are soft but firm.

Tip: This dish can be spruced up further by adding a little bit of spinach, mushroom, or whatever else you might have in the fridge. Be creative!

BREAKFAST HASH PIES

This simple, filling breakfast will make canned hash and cornbread mix staples in your pantry.

COOKING TIME: 35 MINS | SERVINGS: 6

Ingredients:

- 15 oz. can hash (sausage, corned beef, or ham)
- 6 eggs
- Salt and pepper to season
- 8½ oz. package cornbread mix

Directions:

1. Set oven to 400 °F (200 °C) and coat a 12-mold muffin pan with cooking spray.

2. Pour the hash into half of the molds. Use your fingers or a spoon to press it firmly against the base and into the corners so it will form a nice crispy crust.

3. Add an egg on top of each portion of hash; sprinkle with salt and pepper.

4. Prepare the cornbread mix according to the instructions on the box. Divide the dough into six pieces and form each piece into the remaining molds of your muffin pan.

5. Bake for 15-20 minutes. Place the discs of hash on top of the muffins to serve.

Tip: Muffin pans made from silicone rubber are naturally non-stick and flexible, making it easy to get your breakfast out in one piece.

BREAKFASTS

TURKEY MEATBALL AND VEGETABLE HASH

A keto-friendly version of a traditional breakfast favorite.

COOKING TIME: 25 MINS | SERVINGS: 2

INGREDIENTS:

- 8 oz. ground turkey meat
- 1 red sweet pepper, diced
- 6 oz. spinach
- 2 eggs
- 1 lb. cauliflower rice

DIRECTIONS:

1. Heat 2 generous spoonfuls of oil in a large skillet. Wrap the cauliflower (fresh or thawed) in a piece of muslin cloth and wring as much moisture out of it as possible (otherwise it will tend to stick to the pan and remain soggy instead of crisping up).

2. Fry the cauliflower over medium heat with salt and pepper to taste. Press the cauliflower down to the base to create a crust at the bottom. Let it cook for about 5 minutes, then break it up and stir it with your spatula before compacting it again. Repeat this process until your cauliflower starts to brown.

3. While the cauliflower is frying, mix the turkey meat with seasonings of your choice and form it into small balls. Cook these balls in a separate pan on fairly high heat until the turkey is browned and fully done (approx. 8-10 minutes in total).

4. Remove the meatballs to a warm plate. Using the same pan, saute the diced red pepper at a high temperature for 5-6 minutes (Note: it's fine if the edges start blackening slightly). Once the pepper begins to saute, add the spinach and allow it to wilt. This takes no more than a minute or two.

5. At around the time you're halfway through cooking the peppers, add a little oil to a third non-stick pan on medium heat. Once it's hot, crack the eggs into this third pan and let them cook until the yolks are set.

6. For the best presentation, place a bed of cauliflower rice on each plate and cover with the vegetable mix. Then, add a few meatballs and top it all off with a fried egg. Bon appetit!

BREAKFASTS

QUINOA, OATMEAL-STYLE

A much, much healthier alternative to sugary brand-name cereals.

COOKING TIME: 15 MINS | SERVINGS: 1

INGREDIENTS:

- ¼ cup white quinoa
- 1 tbsp. coconut cream
- Your choice of garnishes

DIRECTIONS:

1. Using a sieve or fine colander, rinse the quinoa under a tap – this removes the bitterness.
2. Boil your quinoa in 2 cups of water for approximately 13 minutes, then drain.
3. Stir in the coconut cream and serve with berries, granola, yogurt, nuts, or whatever takes your fancy.

Tip: Toasting quinoa before adding the water gives it an attractive, slightly nutty flavor.

BREAKFASTS

CITRUSY FRENCH TOAST

These are just fine to eat on their own, but can also be served with maple syrup or fruit jelly.

COOKING TIME: 25 MINS | SERVINGS: 6

Ingredients:

- 12 slices of bread
- 8 oz. container cream cheese
- 4 eggs
- 2 tbsp. milk
- ¾ cup orange marmalade

Directions:

1. Cover six of the bread slices with a generous layer of cream cheese, then spread some marmalade over the cream cheese. Place each of the remaining six slices on top of the spread slices to form a sandwich.

2. Beat the eggs and milk until frothy.

3. Melt a pat of butter in a non-stick pan. Dunk each sandwich into the beaten egg and milk mixture, covering the whole exterior. (Note: do not soak the bread too much.)

4. Fry the sandwiches for around 3 minutes before flipping and toasting the other side for the same amount of time. You should see the sides developing a lovely brown color.

5. Serve immediately with honey or whatever other topping you prefer.

Tip: The best kind of bread for French toast is dry but not stale, not sliced too thickly, and without a hard crust.

BREAKFASTS

EASY HOMEMADE DONUTS

Since preparing to deep-fried anything (and cleaning up afterward) is a bit of a chore, you may as well make a big batch of these. You and your family will be glad you did!

COOKING TIME: 25 MINS | SERVINGS: 10

INGREDIENTS:

- Oil for deep-frying
- 12 oz. tubes unbaked flaky biscuits
- ½ cup jam or jelly
- ¾ cup powdered sugar

DIRECTIONS:

1. Heat about 2" of oil in a saucepan or fryer to 350 °F (180 °C).

2. Remove the biscuits from their containers. Gently pry them apart and squash them a little thinner using the palm of your hand.

3. Fry no more than a couple biscuits at once (approx. 1 minute per side). You should see the biscuits puffing up and changing color. When done, place the biscuits on a paper towel to get rid of excess grease.

4. Prepare a pastry bag by attaching a fine nozzle and filling it with jelly. Make sure that all the air has been pressed out before using a paring knife to stab a small hole in the edge of each biscuit, inserting the piping nozzle, and pumping the hole full of jelly.

5. Dust the donuts with sugar and serve.

BREAKFASTS

CHEESY HOMEMADE MUFFINS

Kind of like breakfast hors d'oeuvres, these are always a hit at picnics.

COOKING TIME: 30 MINS | SERVINGS: 10

Ingredients:

- 12 oz. tube unbaked buttermilk biscuit dough
- 8 oz. breakfast sausages
- 2 eggs
- ½ cup cheese, grated
- 3 tbsp. scallions, chopped

Directions:

1. Pre-heat oven to 400 °F (200 °C).

2. Separate the biscuits carefully and flatten them until they're about 5" in diameter. Take a muffin tray and use the dough rounds to line 10 molds.

3. Slice the sausages into bite-sized portions and cook in a pan. Once they're done, place a few pieces on each biscuit.

4. Whisk together the eggs, cheese, and scallions, along with some salt and pepper to taste. Pour a few tbsp. of this mixture into each muffin mold.

5. Bake until the eggs are solid, with a little color on top (approx. 15 minutes).

Tip: If cooking for vegetarians, the sausages can easily be replaced with mushrooms or any plant-based sausage substitute.

BREAKFASTS

BANANA FLAPJACKS

Even the most finicky kids love to eat fresh fruit – as long as it comes in the form of dessert for breakfast…

COOKING TIME: 30 MINS | SERVINGS: 15

INGREDIENTS:

- 2 medium bananas
- 1 egg
- 1¾ cup milk – chocolate, plain, or a mixture of the two
- 16 oz. pancake mix
- Additional garnishes like peanut butter or chocolate chips, maple syrup, etc.

DIRECTIONS:

1. Mash the bananas (the riper, the better) with a fork (Note: this should give you about one cup's worth). Stir together with the milk and egg and then combine with the pancake mix. Be careful not to make the mixture too runny. If using chocolate or peanut butter chips, stir these in as well.

2. Grease and heat a large non-stick pan. Drop in large spoonfuls of the batter, making 3-4 pancakes at a time. Flip each around 30 seconds after you see bubbles appearing on the top, then cook the bottom for about another minute and a half.

3. Serve hot with syrup, berries, and other garnishes on the side.

Tip: If you want to switch things up, buy a selection of frozen fruit pulps and thaw before using as you would the mashed banana.

BREAKFASTS

CHICKEN SANDWICHES FOR BRUNCH

These delectable sandwiches take a while to get ready but don't require much effort – why not make a fruit salad and some pancakes while they're cooking in the oven?

COOKING TIME: 35 MINS | SERVINGS: 8

Ingredients:

- 16 oz. tube uncooked buttermilk biscuit dough
- 8 frozen, boneless, breaded chicken tenders
- 4 eggs
- 2 tbsp. milk
- ½ cup maple syrup

Directions:

1. Set oven to 350 °F (180 °C) and allow a few minutes for it to get hot.

2. Remove the biscuits from their packaging, separate them, and place them on a baking sheet. Bake according to the directions on the box.

3. Increase the temperature to 425 °F (220 °C) before taking out the biscuits. Bake the chicken tenders until fully done (approx. 12-15 minutes).

4. While the chicken is baking, beat together the eggs and milk, along with salt and pepper to taste. Pour this mixture into a hot skillet and scramble. Take the scrabbled eggs off the heat as soon as they're no longer runny.

5. Stack them up: use a biscuit as a base, cover it with some scrambled eggs topped with a chicken tender, and drip a little syrup over the whole stack.

NO-CARB HAM-AND-HOLLANDAISE CUPS

A keto-friendly version of the classic Eggs Benedict.

COOKING TIME: 25 MINS | SERVINGS: 2

Ingredients:

- 4 egg tortillas
- 6 tbsp. butter
- 4 eggs plus 2 yolks
- 1 tbsp. lemon juice
- 4 pieces dry-cured ham

Directions:

1. Scrunch down the egg wraps into the cups of a muffin tray (Note: depending on the brand and size of your muffin molds, you may have to trim the wraps a bit). Bake at 300 °F (150 °C) for approximately 12 minutes (Note: the wraps should come out dry, a little crispy, and no longer flexible).

2. Knowing how to make hollandaise sauce instantly makes you a better cook, and it's not actually that hard. Simply place the lemon juice, egg yolks (at room temperature), and a pinch of salt in a blender. Melt the butter on low heat or in the microwave. With the blender running, add the melted butter very slowly – drop by drop is ideal. The sauce should congeal as if by magic (Note: you can add a tsp. of water if it comes out too thick).

3. The easiest way to poach eggs is with a microwave-safe poaching bowl. If you want to go the traditional route, add several inches of salted water and a dash of vinegar to a pot, bring it to a low simmer, stir the water until it twirls, then carefully crack each egg into it. Let them cook for 3-4 minutes, then remove with a slotted spoon.

4. To serve, line the egg wrap cups with slices of ham, place an egg on top, and spoon a blob of hollandaise sauce over the egg.

Tips: If you prefer to cook from scratch, you can make very thin omelets from a watery mixture instead of using store-bought egg wraps.

BREAKFASTS

EGG-AND-BACON TACOS

Who said a traditional breakfast has to be served on a plate?

COOKING TIME: 20 MINS | SERVINGS: 2

INGREDIENTS:

- 4 rashers bacon
- 6 eggs
- 4 corn taco shells
- Red salsa
- 1 avocado, sliced

DIRECTIONS:

1. Cook the bacon in a large skillet on a medium heat until it's brown and crispy.

2. While the bacon is frying, beat the eggs thoroughly with a whisk or fork.

3. Remove the bacon from the pan and add the eggs to the grease it has left behind. Don't stop stirring the eggs – the idea is to create smooth, consistent scrambled eggs instead of individual chunks. Add salt and pepper to taste once the eggs are done.

4. Heat the tortillas and salsa in the microwave. Put together your tacos and add some salsa and avocado before serving.

SNACKS AND HORS D'OEUVRES

SNACKS AND HORS D'OEUVRES

SPIRAL PIZZAS

A lifesaver for any parent, these can be made in large batches and frozen for future after-school snacking.

COOKING TIME: 35 MINS | SERVINGS: 24

Ingredients:

- ½ lb. lean mince, beef
- 8 oz. can Italian tomato sauce
- ½ cup mozzarella cheese, grated
- Dried oregano to taste
- 16 oz. tubes crescent roll dough

Directions:

1. Set oven to 375 °F (190 °C) and leave it to warm up while you prepare the other ingredients.

2. Cook the mince in a pan until browned, adding salt and pepper to taste.

3. Pour off the fat in the pan and then mix the tomato sauce, cheese, and oregano in with the meat.

4. Cut the dough into squares. Spoon a generous amount of filling onto the bottom edge of each, then roll up from the bottom, as tightly as you can without squishing out the meat sauce. Slice each roll into bite-sized spirals.

5. Bake for 15 minutes.

SNACKS AND HORS D'OEUVRES

SWEET POTATO AND BLUE CHEESE POUTINE

A clever twist on this underrated Canadian favorite. The slight sweetness of the jam complements the robust flavor of blue cheese.

COOKING TIME: 25 MINS | SERVINGS: 2

Ingredients:

- 1 tbsp. olive oil
- 2 large sweet potatoes
- 1 tbsp. apricot jam
- 3 tbsp. blue cheese, crumbled

Directions:

1. Peel the sweet potatoes (if you like) and cut into ½" strips.

2. Place a large non-stick pan on medium heat and fry the sweet potato strips in the oil. Stir the strips every now and then so that all the sides brown evenly. Add salt to taste.

3. After approximately 15 minutes, take the now-tender sweet potatoes off the heat. Stir in the jam and sprinkle the cheese over before serving.

SNACKS AND HORS D'OEUVRES

SIMPLE HUMMUS

Snacks are nice, but snacks with a classic dip can be awesome.

COOKING TIME: 5 MINS | SERVINGS: 1½ CUPS

INGREDIENTS:

- ¾ cup canola oil
- 16 oz. can garbanzo beans
- 3 tbsp. lemon juice
- 2 tsp. minced garlic
- ½ tsp. salt

DIRECTIONS:

1. Drain and rinse the garbanzo beans.

2. Toss all ingredients into a food processor and let it whiz until you have a smooth consistency.

3. Scrape the mixture into a bowl and serve with carrot sticks, tortilla chips, pita bread, or whatever snack foods you prefer.

Tip: If you happen to have some, ½ cup tahini (sesame seed paste) will add a huge amount of flavor to this dipping sauce.

SNACKS AND HORS D'OEUVRES

CALIFORNIA CRAB PUFFS

This appetizer can be served hot or cold. Baking instead of deep-frying the puffs cuts down the greasiness.

COOKING TIME: 30 MINS | SERVINGS: 12

Ingredients:

- 12 wonton wrappers
- 4 oz. cream cheese, softened
- 4 tbsp. mayonnaise
- 6 oz. can crab meat
- ¼ cup chopped scallions

Directions:

1. Pre-heat the oven to 350 °F (175 °C).

2. Apply cooking spray to a muffin tin with small molds. Line the inside of each with the wonton wrappers to create a cup. Bake these for about 6 minutes.

3. Drain the canned crab, then use a fork to fluff the meat and remove any bony bits.

4. Whisk the mayonnaise and cream cheese together until no lumps remain. Add the crab meat and scallions along with salt and pepper to taste.

5. Place a generous spoonful of the crab mixture into each wonton cup. Return to the oven for another 12 minutes.

Tip: Real crab meat is pretty expensive. "Crab sticks" or "surimi" is actually white fish processed to taste like crab; it's much cheaper and somewhat less tasty, but the average dinner guest probably won't mind it.

SNACKS AND HORS D'OEUVRES

MINIATURE BAGUETTES WITH HONEY-AND-CHILI DIP

This dipping sauce combines the sweetness of honey and the smoothness of ricotta with a little bit of spice. Crusty bread provides some texture to round out the experience.

COOKING TIME: 15 MINS | SERVINGS: 6

Ingredients:

- 9½ oz. package par-baked mini-baguettes
- ½ cup honey
- 2 tsp. chili flakes
- 16 oz. tub ricotta cheese
- Fresh herbs to taste, minced

Directions:

1. Bake the mini-baguettes according to the instructions on the packaging.

2. While the baguettes are baking, bring the honey and chili flakes to a light boil in a small pot and let the spice release its flavor for about 5 minutes. Stir every now and then.

3. Allow the honey to cool completely. Once it is at room temperature, strain it through a sieve to remove the chili. Whisk the mixture along with the ricotta and herbs until it reaches a feathery consistency – an electric mixer is your best friend at this point.

4. To serve, place the dipping sauce in a bowl on a wooden board and arrange the mini-baguettes around it.

SNACKS AND HORS D'OEUVRES

BRAISED PORK NACHOS

Known as "carnitas con chifles" in Spanish, this recipe uses plantain chips instead of toasted tortilla wedges.

COOKING TIME: 15 MINS | SERVINGS: 4

INGREDIENTS:

- 12 oz. package braised pork (carnitas)
- 5 oz. bag of plantain chips
- 1 cup grated cheddar cheese
- ½ cup guacamole
- 2/3 cup red salsa

DIRECTIONS:

1. Place some parchment paper or foil onto a baking sheet; set oven to 450 °F (230 °C).

2. Heat the carnitas in the microwave until warm.

3. Assemble your nachos by spreading the plantain chips over the parchment paper and top with the carnitas and cheddar.

4. Let it heat in the oven for 5 minutes, or until the cheese is thoroughly melted.

5. To serve, transfer the nachos to a plate and add spoonfuls of salsa and guacamole at random.

SNACKS AND HORS D'OEUVRES

CHEESY STICKS

These are great to nibble on while binge-watching your favorite TV series, and can be stored for several days in an airtight container.

COOKING TIME: 35 MINS | SERVINGS: 36

INGREDIENTS:

- ½ cup butter, at room temperature
- 2 cups cheese, grated
- 1¼ cups flour
- Salt and chili powder to taste

DIRECTIONS:

1. Pre-heat oven to 350 °F (175 °C).

2. Using an electric mixer, whisk the butter until it has a feathery texture. Add the cheese and stir. Then, add the dry ingredients and beat until smooth.

3. Form the dough into a sheet of about 6" by 15". Slice into strips of around ¼-½" wide.

4. Space the strips evenly on a lined baking sheet. Bake for 15-20 minutes, or until they turn a golden color.

5. Remove from the oven and allow the strips to cool on the baking sheet for 5 minutes. Then, transfer the strips to a wire tray to ventilate them while they cool completely.

SNACKS AND HORS D'OEUVRES

ASIAN CHICKEN TARTLETS

Rotisserie chicken is sometimes a godsend. Combine it with a little seasoning and dress it up in a cute package, and you have a special snack that's actually not all that difficult to prepare.

COOKING TIME: 30 MINS | SERVINGS: 36

INGREDIENTS:

- 1½ cups cooked chicken
- ½ cup ranch-style salad dressing
- 1¼ oz. packet chili seasoning
- 36 wonton wrappers
- 1 cup cheese, grated

DIRECTIONS:

1. Set oven to 350 °F (175 °C) and leave it to heat up while you prepare your ingredients.

2. Shred the chicken using two forks. Make sure to remove any small bones and pieces of cartilage as you shred.

3. Stir the seasoning into the dressing, then pour the dressing over the shredded chicken and stir.

4. Apply cooking spray to a muffin tin. Form the wonton wrappers into cups in the molds and bake until slightly crispy (approx. 5 minutes).

5. Fill each pastry cup with a spoonful of the chicken mixture. Top with cheese.

6. Return to the oven for another 10 minutes.

7. Serve immediately. If you like, you can garnish the tartlets with chopped scallions and sour cream.

SNACKS AND HORS D'OEUVRES

CARAMEL APPLE AND BRIE KABOBS

Fruit and certain cheeses get along like a house on fire.

COOKING TIME: 10 MINS | SERVINGS: 6

Ingredients:

- 2 honeycrisp or golden delicious apples
- 6 oz. brie cheese
- ½ cup hot caramel ice cream topping
- ½ cup crushed nuts – cashew, macadamia, or mixed
- 2 tbsp. dried cherries or cranberries, chopped

Directions:

1. Soak your skewers in water for at least half an hour to prevent them from splintering.

2. Core the apples, then cut them and the cheese into cubes.

3. Assemble the skewers by switching between pieces of cheese and apple. Pour over the caramel sauce and top with nuts and berries.

SNACKS AND HORS D'OEUVRES

CHEESY BROCCOLI DIP

Broccoli really doesn't deserve its bad reputation. Prepared right, it can easily hold its own.

COOKING TIME: 35 MINS | SERVINGS: 3 cups

Ingredients:

- 4 cups broccoli florets
- 2 cups sour cream
- ½ cup cheddar, grated
- 1 oz. vegetable stock powder

Directions:

1. Set oven to 350 °F (175 °C) and coat a mid-sized casserole dish with cooking spray.

2. Using a food processor, pulse the broccoli a few times. Alternatively, use a knife and chop the broccoli into small enough pieces that are suitable for a dipping sauce.

3. Scrape the broccoli into a microwaveable bowl, along with a few tsp. water, and microwave for 3-4 minutes until it's just blanched (i.e., slightly tender but not fully cooked).

4. Stir the sour cream, stock powder, and cheese together until you achieve a smooth consistency. Add the broccoli to the mixture and combine.

5. Pour the mixture into the casserole dish and top with additional cheddar. Leave in the oven, uncovered, for about 25 minutes. Serve with cheesy sticks, nacho chips, or raw sliced vegetables.

SNACKS AND HORS D'OEUVRES

DIET-BUSTING CHOCO-COCO BALLS

A perfect sweet treat for those hot summer months when you just can't bring yourself to turn on the oven.

COOKING TIME: 25 MINS | SERVINGS: 6

Ingredients:

- 8 oz. unsweetened dried coconut
- ¼ cup coconut oil
- 2 tbsp. maple syrup
- 1 tsp. vanilla extract
- ¼ cup chocolate chips

Directions:

1. Throw all the ingredients except the chocolate chips and one-quarter of the coconut oil into a food processor (Note: if the coconut oil has congealed, put it in the microwave for a few seconds to melt). Using the pulse setting, process the ingredients just enough to form a kind of batter that you can mold with your hands.

2. Place the chocolate chips and remaining oil into a small saucepan and stir constantly while the chocolate melts over very low heat or, ideally, a bain-marie (i.e., a bowl placed over a saucepan containing a few inches of boiling water).

3. Form the coconut mixture into balls of about 1-1½" wide. Arrange these balls on a sheet of parchment paper.

4. Pour the melted chocolate over the coconut balls. Let them cool naturally, or have them set in the fridge for a few minutes if you just can't wait.

SNACKS AND HORS D'OEUVRES

GREEK PIZZETTAS

Simple pizza-like snacks with a nice kick of herby flavor.

COOKING TIME: 20 MINS | SERVINGS: 4

Ingredients:

- 2 English muffins
- 2 tbsp. cream cheese
- 4 tsp. pesto
- Half a red onion
- ¼ cup feta cheese

Directions:

1. Pre-heat oven to 425 °F (220 °C).

2. Slice the muffins in half and arrange on a baking sheet.

3. Combine the pesto and cream cheese. Spread this mixture onto the muffin slices.

4. Thinly slice the onion and layer the slices over the pesto and cream cheese. Crumble the feta cheese over this.

5. Bake until the cheese shows some color (approx. 7 minutes).

SNACKS AND HORS D'OEUVRES

POOR MAN'S CHOCOLATE ECLAIRS

Even if you've never baked a cookie in your life, this is one recipe you should have no trouble with.

COOKING TIME: 20 MINS | SERVINGS: 10

INGREDIENTS:

- 12 oz. tube unbaked buttermilk biscuit dough
- 1.55 oz. chocolate candy bar (any brand)
- 2 tsp. sugar
- Pinch of cinnamon

DIRECTIONS:

1. Pre-heat oven to 450 °F (230 °C).

2. Pull the biscuits apart and roll them out until each is about 3" across.

3. Cut the candy bar into 10 pieces. Place one piece on each portion of biscuit dough. Fold the dough over to enclose the chocolate inside. It should make a rough ball that is pinched together at one end.

4. Arrange the balls pinched side down on a baking sheet (Note: the balls should not be placed too close together). Dust with sugar and cinnamon.

5. Bake for approximately 10 minutes, or until you see the balls start to change color.

SNACKS AND HORS D'OEUVRES

HOT OLIVE DIP

This cheeky relish can be served with crackers or breadsticks as an appetizer, or as a sauce for roast vegetables, burgers, and more.

COOKING TIME: 10 MINUTES | SERVINGS: 2 CUPS

Ingredients:

- 16 oz. jar pickled pepperoncini
- 7 oz. jar pimiento-stuffed olives
- 1 shallot
- 1 tbsp. French mustard

Directions:

1. Peel and roughly chop the shallot and then drain off the olive and pepper juices.

2. Place all the ingredients in a blender or food processor and whiz until your desired consistency is achieved.

POULTRY

POULTRY

THANKSGIVING MONDAY DINNER

Few families can finish an entire turkey in one sitting. You don't need to limit yourself to sandwiches when using up the leftovers.

COOKING TIME: 20 MINS | SERVINGS: 4

INGREDIENTS:

- 10 oz. uncooked penne pasta
- 4 oz. butter
- 1 oz. ranch salad dressing powder
- 1 cup frozen peas and carrots, thawed
- 3 cups leftover turkey, diced

DIRECTIONS:

1. Set a pot filled with plenty of salted water on the stove. Once it's boiling vigorously, add the penne and cook for 10-12 minutes until the pasta is tender but not mushy.

2. Melt the butter in a large saucepan. Sprinkle in the ranch seasoning and stir well. Add the vegetables and fry until cooked but still crunchy (approx. 3 minutes).

3. Drain the pasta in a colander before tossing it into the pan with the carrots, peas, and turkey. Cook together for another 3 minutes, stirring occasionally. Heat to serving temperature and serve.

LOW-CARB CHICKEN ENCHILADAS

Jicama is a Mexican root vegetable not widely known north of the border. Tortillas that made from it are every bit as good as those consisting of corn or wheat flour, yet contain very few carbohydrates.

COOKING TIME: 45 MINS | SERVINGS: 4

INGREDIENTS:

- 6 chicken tenders
- Salt and pepper to taste
- 1 cup enchilada or taco sauce
- 7½ oz. package jicama wraps
- 1 cup cheese, grated

DIRECTIONS:

1. Pre-heat oven to 350 °F (175 °C).

2. Season the chicken tenders with salt and pepper and arrange them on a baking dish. Place the tenders in the oven for 25 minutes, or until they're no longer pink in the middle.

3. Once the chicken is cooked, break the meat in to slivers in a mixing bowl.

4. Coat the base of a casserole pan with about 1 tbsp. of the enchilada or taco sauce.

5. Spoon a small amount of chicken onto the middle of each wrap. Roll it into a tube and place in the casserole pan.

6. Pour the rest of the sauce over the enchiladas and top with cheese. Return to the oven for 20 minutes before serving.

POULTRY

TURKEY BREAST WITH HONEY-MUSTARD GLAZE

Chicken, duck, and turkey all appreciate a little bit of sweetness to complement their natural flavor.

COOKING TIME: 2¾ HOURS | SERVINGS: 12

Ingredients:

- ¾ cup apple or orange juice concentrate
- 1/3 cup honey
- Salt and pepper to taste
- 1 tbsp. mustard powder
- 1 turkey breast, not deboned

Directions:

1. Pre-heat oven to 325 °F (160 °C).

2. Pour the concentrated juice, honey, and seasonings into a small pot. Heat slowly for 2-3 minutes, stirring continuously.

3. Place the turkey breast on top of a wire rack in a baking dish, skin side up. Season with salt and pepper and coat with the glaze.

4. Bake for 2-2½ hours, spooning over the liquid that collects at the bottom of the dish every half an hour.

5. Once the turkey is done (Note: you can confirm this with a meat thermometer inserted into the center of the breast – it should measure a temperature of 170 °F), remove it, cover it with foil, and let it rest for 15 minutes.

6. Carve and serve.

BASIL CHICKEN SPAGHETTI

Almost no genuine Italian pasta dishes contain chicken, but there's no reason to be a slave to authenticity.

COOKING TIME: 25 MINUTES | SERVINGS: 4

Ingredients:

- 4 deboned chicken breasts
- 6 oz. basil pesto
- 16 oz. uncooked spaghetti
- 1 cup cherry tomatoes
- 2 tbsp. soffritto seasoning powder

Directions:

1. The night before, place the chicken breasts on a cutting board and slice into cutlets. Toss with the pesto and transfer to a Ziplock bag. Leave the bag of chicken in the fridge to marinate overnight.

2. Fill a large pot with water, add several tbsp. salt, and wait for it to boil.

3. While you wait for the water to boil, heat some oil in a large skillet. Add the marinated chicken and cook until firm (approx. 5 minutes each side).

4. Remove the chicken and place the tomatoes, sliced in half, in the pan with additional olive oil, along with the seasoning mix. Once the pasta is done (approx. 8 minutes), drain it in a colander, add to the pan along with the chicken, and mix thoroughly before serving.

Tip: There's nothing wrong with using seasoning mix, but genuine Italian soffritto isn't all that hard to make. Simply stir-fry one cup onion with half a cup each of celery and carrots in a little olive oil and garlic.

COUNTRY-STYLE CHICKEN PIE

This upscale meal requires little effort to prepare, making it perfect for entertaining on weeknights.

COOKING TIME: 40 MINUTES | SERVINGS: 4

INGREDIENTS:

- 2 cups rotisserie chicken, diced
- 8 oz. packet spinach
- 6 oz. brie cheese
- ¼ cup toasted, chopped nuts (walnuts or pecans)
- 1x 9" (5 oz.) sheet pie dough

DIRECTIONS:

1. Pre-heat oven to 475 °F (250 °C), with the oven rack in the middle position.

2. Let the spinach thaw, and press out as much water as possible. Chop 1/3 of the cheese fairly finely.

3. In a microwave-safe bowl, combine the spinach, chopped cheese, chicken, salt and pepper to taste, and a few tbsp. water. Cover with clingfilm (Note: poke a few holes in this with a fork), and microwave on high until warm.

4. If necessary, roll out the pie dough until it's about ⅛" thick and roughly circular. Transfer the dough to a baking sheet covered with baking paper.

5. Spoon a layer of filling over the pie – round up to about 1" from the rim. Use your fingers to fold over the remaining edge, pinching the dough together as you go.

6. Slice the remaining brie cheese into generous chunks and space them on top of the pie, rind side up.

7. Cook in the oven for approximately 15 minutes, or until the cheese melts. Let the pie rest for 5 minutes before serving.

POULTRY

INDIVIDUAL CHICKEN CALZONES

Folding over the pizza base to create a pocket for the topping seals in moisture and flavor, leading to a juicier, more succulent result.

COOKING TIME: 45 MINUTES | SERVINGS: 4

Ingredients:

- 1 lb. pizza dough
- 2 cups cooked chicken, finely chopped
- 2 cups cheddar, grated
- 5.2 oz. tub cream cheese with garlic and herbs
- 1/3 cup black olives, pitted and sliced

Directions:

1. Pre-heat oven to 475 °F (250 °C), with the oven rack in the middle. Take the dough out of the fridge to let it heat up to room temperature before working with it.

2. Place a sheet of parchment paper on a baking sheet.

3. Mix together the cheeses, chicken, and olives. Add salt and pepper to taste.

4. Separate the dough into four equal pieces. Roll out each into an 8" circle.

5. Divide the filling between the dough rounds. Cover one half of each up to about 1" from the edge.

6. Fold over the dough and pinch shut. Brush the top with olive oil and slice two small holes in the top to allow steam to escape.

7. Bake for about 20 minutes, or until the top begins to brown. Let the calzones rest for 5 minutes before serving.

CITRUS CHICKEN WITH ASPARAGUS

Assuming that you don't mind the carbs, this saucy chicken dish goes well with brown rice.

COOKING TIME: 30 MINUTES | SERVINGS: 2

INGREDIENTS:

- 4 chicken thighs, deboned but with skin on
- 2 tbsp. lemon juice
- 1½ tsp. capers
- 1½ pounds thick asparagus stalks
- 1 cup chicken stock

DIRECTIONS:

Chicken:

1. Season the thighs with salt and pepper to taste.

2. Place the thighs, skin side down, in a very hot heavy-bottomed skillet over medium heat with some oil. Cook for about 8 minutes before turning and cooking for another 4 minutes. The skin should be brown and crisp; if not, give it a few more minutes on the skin side.

3. Remove the chicken from the pan and keep warm.

Sauce:

4. Pour the excess grease from the pan and add the chicken stock. Scrape the bottom with a spatula to release the fond (i.e., the flavorful brown substance sticking to the bottom of the pan).

5. Add the lemon juice and capers; simmer until half the liquid remains. Throw in a dash of olive oil and seasonings of your choice.

Asparagus:

6. Slice or snap off the woody bottom part of each stalk while waiting for a saucepan half-filled with salted water to boil. Add some ice cubes to a separate bowl of cold water.

7. Boil the asparagus for around 3 minutes before transferring the stalks to the bowl of cold water to stop the cooking process. Each stalk should be deep green in color but still crunchy.

8. Add the asparagus to the simmering sauce and serve once warm. Top with a portion of chicken drizzled with extra sauce.

CHICKEN WITH HERBY QUINOA

Cooking quinoa perfectly remains a mystery to many people. Using pre-cooked packages takes a lot of the guesswork out of this process.

COOKING TIME: 20 MINUTES | SERVINGS: 2

Ingredients:

- 2 chicken breasts, bones and skin removed
- 16 oz. parboiled quinoa
- 2 cups broccoli florets
- 1 cup cherry tomatoes, halved
- ¼ cup basil pesto

Directions:

1. Place the chicken on your chopping board between two pieces of saran wrap. Pound the chicken flat with a rolling pin or mallet (Note: this is not to tenderize the breasts, but to make them cook more quickly). Season with salt and pepper to taste.

2. Heat a few tsp. oil in a medium-sized skillet and add the broccoli florets. Stir-fry for 5 minutes over high heat before adding in the cherry tomatoes. Season with salt and pepper once the skin of the tomatoes gets wrinkled. Transfer to a serving dish covered with tinfoil.

3. Place the pan back onto the stove. Add a little more oil and the flattened chicken breasts. Cook for about 5 minutes, turn, and then cook for an additional 3 minutes on lower heat. Transfer to the serving dish along with the broccoli.

4. Place the pre-cooked quinoa in the pan along with the pesto and a dash of salt. Add boiling water according to the instructions on the packaging.

5. Once done, fluff the quinoa with a fork and spoon onto two plates. Cover this with the vegetables and top with chicken sliced into strips.

GARLICKY CHICKEN SANDWICHES

Pasta sauce on a hot sandwich may seem like a wonky idea, but it works surprisingly well.

COOKING TIME: 30 MINUTES | SERVINGS: 4

INGREDIENTS:

- 2 chicken breasts, deboned
- 1 cup garlic breadcrumbs
- 1 cup garlic-and-herb pasta sauce
- 1 cup mozzarella, grated
- 4 crusty bread rolls

DIRECTIONS:

1. Pre-heat oven to 400 °F (200 °C).

2. Lay the chicken breasts on a chopping board after removing the skin. Pressing down with your palm, carefully slice each breast horizontally using a sharp knife. Place each half between two sheets of plastic wrap and pound flat with a rolling pin or kitchen mallet.

3. Pour the breadcrumbs into a wide bowl. Press the chicken pieces into the crumbs to coat.

4. Place the chicken pieces on a lined baking sheet and bake for approximately 20 minutes, or until cooked through.

5. Coat each piece of chicken with a generous spoonful of pasta sauce and top with cheese. Return to the oven until the cheese has melted. Place on buttered rolls to serve.

POULTRY

FAUX-BBQ CHICKEN

In winter, or if you live in an apartment, grilling isn't always an option. That doesn't mean you have to give up on preparing your favorite dishes at home, or at least passable replicas of them.

COOKING TIME: 35 MINUTES | SERVINGS: 4

Ingredients:

- 1 chicken, portioned
- 2 cups BBQ sauce
- 1½ cups onions, diced
- 1 large green bell pepper, chopped

Directions:

1. Add a few tsp. oil to a pressure cooker on medium heat and brown the chicken portions. When the portions have gained some color, add the onions, pepper, and sauce. Toss the chicken so the sauce covers it completely.

2. Close the lid of the cooker and insert the pressure regulator. Cook for 10-15 minutes before taking the pressure cooker off the heat. Leave for approximately 15 minutes – the chicken will continue to cook as the pressure slowly falls. Serve with biscuits and a salad.

CHICKEN SKEWERS

Grilled kabobs are already great, but a little marinade can make them amazing.

COOKING TIME: 30 MINUTES | SERVINGS: 4

Ingredients:

- 1 lb. chicken breasts, deboned and skinless
- 1 red bell pepper
- 1 medium zucchini
- 1 red onion
- 2/3 cup vinaigrette salad dressing

Directions:

1. Soak bamboo or wooden skewers in water for at least half an hour to prevent them from splintering.

2. Cut the chicken, zucchini, and pepper into 1½" pieces. Slice the onion into quarters. Pour half of the salad dressing over the ingredients, stirring to cover everything completely. Place in the fridge for an hour to overnight.

3. Assemble the kabobs, alternating pieces of onion, pepper, zucchini, and chicken.

4. Grill the kabobs on a barbecue or broil in the oven on medium heat (Note: the chicken should be done and no longer pink in the center after approx. 9 minutes). Turn the kabobs and brush with the remaining vinaigrette as needed.

POULTRY

SAVORY WAFFLES WITH CHICKEN

Who would have thought that a waffle iron can be useful for more than dessert?

COOKING TIME: 30 MINUTES | SERVINGS: 8

Ingredients:

- ½ cup red onion
- ½ cup mushrooms
- 1 cup cooked chicken, cut into strips
- 1 cup grated cheddar
- 17.3 oz. package puff pastry

Directions:

1. Take the puff pastry out of the freezer and leave to thaw.

2. Chop the vegetables and chicken.

3. Fry the onion in a little oil over medium heat until translucent. Turn the heat down slightly and cook the onions until browned, then add the mushrooms. Cook for another 3 minutes. Allow to cool, then stir in the chicken and cheese.

4. Turn on your waffle iron and wait for it to get hot. Unroll the puff pastry and divide it into rectangles that are a little larger than your waffle molds.

5. Spoon a couple of heaped tbsp. of the chicken mixture into the center of each dough square. Fold the corners inwards, pressing the edges together to close.

6. Grill the pastry pockets in the waffle iron until crisp (approx. 7 minutes).

FRAGRANT CHICKEN WITH CAULIFLOWER RICE

"Spicy" doesn't have to mean "hot". Likewise, "cauliflower" doesn't have to mean "boring".

COOKING TIME: 40 MINUTES | SERVINGS: 4

INGREDIENTS:

- 8 chicken thighs, skin and bone not removed
- 4 tsp. whole cumin seeds
- 1 fresh cauliflower
- ½ cup fresh mint, minced
- 5 limes, zested and sliced into wedges

DIRECTIONS:

1. Pre-heat oven to 375 °F (190 °C).

2. Season the chicken with salt and pepper to taste while heating a spoonful of oil in a wide, heavy-bottomed pan. Place the chicken pieces skin-side down and fry until golden-brown in color (approx. 8 minutes). (Note: don't drain the flavorful chicken grease from the pan!)

3. Move the chicken to a baking tray, skin side up this time. Top with half the cumin seeds and bake for 15-20 minutes, until the middle is no longer pink. Remove from the oven and cover the tray with tinfoil.

4. Prepare the cauliflower rice by removing the stem and slicing the cauliflower into ½" pieces. Use your food processor's grater attachment, or pulse the cauliflower in batches until the pieces are about the size of rice grains. Place the chopped cauliflower on a clean kitchen towel and squeeze out all the excess moisture.

5. Heat up the pan in which you browned the chicken again. Once it's very hot, add in the cauliflower rice, along with the remaining cumin, salt, and pepper to taste. Cook while stirring for approximately 8 minutes.

6. Once the cauliflower has softened, take it off the hob and toss with the lime zest and most of the chopped mint. Serve the chicken on a bed of cauliflower, garnished with more mint. Place the lime wedges on the side.

ROAST CHICKEN WITH SPICED YOGURT

Plenty of traditional Indian sauces use yogurt as a base as it allows the flavors to travel and mitigates their heat.

COOKING TIME: 45 MINUTES | SERVINGS: 4

Ingredients:

- 2 lbs. sweet potatoes
- 1 lemon
- ¼ tsp. lemon zest
- 8 chicken thighs, with bones and skin
- ½ cup unflavored, unsweetened yogurt
- 2½ tsp. spice mix

Directions:

1. Pre-heat oven with two wire racks to 450 °F (230 °C). Prepare a baking sheet by lining it with wax paper.

2. Slice the sweet potatoes and lemon into wedges of about 1½" wide. (Note: there's no need to peel the sweet potatoes.) Coat with 2 large spoonful's of oil, salt, and pepper to taste. Arrange the lemon and sweet potatoes on the baking sheet, skin side down Make sure that none of the pieces are touching. Bake on the upper rack of the oven for 30 minutes, or until the sweet potatoes start to turn brown.

3. Season the chicken thighs with salt, pepper, and 2 tsp. spices. Brown the thighs, skin side down, in a hot heavy-based pan for 8-10 minutes before transferring them to a baking dish, skin side up. Roast for another 25 minutes.

4. In a small bowl, stir the yogurt, lemon zest, a pinch of salt, and remaining spice mix together.

5. Remove the chicken from oven, cover with foil, and allow it to cool for a few minutes before serving with the sauce and vegetables.

SEAFOOD & FISH

PEPPERY SALMON FILLETS WITH STRING BEANS

Cooking fish with spices may seem a little odd, but plenty of Greek and Spanish seafood dishes include a healthy dose of smoked paprika.

COOKING TIME: 30 MINUTES | SERVINGS: 4

Ingredients:

- 4x 1"-thick salmon fillets
- 1¼ tsp. smoked paprika powder
- 1 pound string beans
- 6 cloves garlic
- ½ cup pickled pepperoncini peppers

Directions:

1. Peel and crush the garlic. Cut the ends off of the green beans.

2. Season the salmon with ¾ of the paprika, salt, and pepper (Note: leave the skin on the fish, as this will become deliciously crispy). Set a large, heavy-bottomed pan on high heat until very hot. Add a tbsp. oil and sear the fillets, skin side down. Allow the fillets to cook for approximately 6 minutes, then flip and cook the other side for another 4 minutes. Remove to a plate and dust with the rest of the paprika.

3. Add a little more oil to the pan if necessary and stir-fry the beans along with garlic, salt, and pepper to taste. The idea is to slightly char the beans for a deeper flavor.

4. After approximately 6 minutes, add a dash of water, put on the lid, turn down the heat, and allow the beans to steam for another minute.

5. Toss in the pepperoncinis with the beans. Serve the fish on top of a bed of the vegetables.

SEAFOOD & FISH

STEAMED SALMON WITH BUTTERY ASPARAGUS

Although salmon isn't the most delicate fish, it still benefits from a gentle cooking method.

COOKING TIME: 30 MINUTES | SERVINGS: 4

Ingredients:

- 1 lb. asparagus stems
- 4 salmon fillets (1" thick), skin removed
- ½ cup dry white wine
- 2 tbsp. fresh herbs like parsley, chives, or dill
- 3 tbsp. butter

Directions:

1. Snap or cut off the woody stems of the asparagus, then arrange the spears into a kind of lattice in a large pan. Add 1 cup salted water.

2. Season the salmon with salt and pepper to taste. Place on top of the asparagus. Place the lid on the pan and bring the water to a boil.

3. Steam for approximately 8 minutes, or until fish is flaky. When done, remove the asparagus and salmon to a serving tray.

4. Add the wine to the juices in the pan and cook for 5 minutes. Remove from the heat and add the butter, chopped herbs, salt, and pepper to taste. Beat the mixture well before drizzling the sauce over the salmon and vegetables. Serve with lemon wedges on the side.

SEAFOOD & FISH

PAN-FRIED TERIYAKI FISH

A slightly exotic dish that you'd be happy to order at a restaurant but which is surprisingly easy to prepare at home.

COOKING TIME: 20 MINUTES | SERVINGS: 4

Ingredients:

- 24 oz. fish fillets (mahi mahi, cod, or halibut)
- ¼ tsp. garlic powder
- 1 tsp. fresh ginger, grated
- ¼ cup spicy teriyaki sauce

Directions:

1. Blot the fish fillets dry with paper towels, as this will allows the outside to become crisp when frying. Season with salt, pepper, and garlic powder.

2. Add oil to a heavy-bottomed pan and fry the fillets on medium-high heat for approximately 5 minutes per side, or until cooked through. Transfer the fish to a plate and cover with tinfoil.

3. Return the pan to the heat and cook the grated ginger for about a minute. Add the teriyaki sauce and heat while stirring and scraping the bottom. Drizzle over the fish to serve.

SEAFOOD & FISH

BREADED FLOUNDER

A weeknight staple that can be made with almost any kind of fish.

COOKING TIME: 25 MINUTES | SERVINGS: 6

INGREDIENTS:

- ¾ cup panko breadcrumbs
- ½ cup pecorino cheese, finely grated
- 2 eggs
- 2 tbsp. milk
- 2 lbs. flounder fillets

DIRECTIONS:

1. Pre-heat oven to 450 °F (230 °C). Coat a baking tray with cooking spray.

2. Beat the eggs and milk together.

3. Mix the cheese, panko, salt, and pepper in a plastic bag.

4. Bathe the flounder pieces in the egg mixture before placing them in the bag. Shake the bag to coat the fish with the breading.

5. Bake for 15 minutes, or until the fish has a firm, flaky texture.

POISSON EN PAPILLOTE WITH ROAST POTATOES

"Posson en papillote" is French for "fish in foil". Baking fish in this way allows the various flavors to mingle and infuse the fish.

COOKING TIME: 45 MINUTES | SERVINGS: 4

Ingredients:

- 1½ pounds fingerling or new potatoes, sliced in half
- 8 oz. cherry tomatoes, sliced in half
- 4 fish fillets, 1" thick (halibut, mahi-mahi, swordfish, striped bass, or whatever you prefer)
- 1 lemon, sliced thinly
- 2 tbsp. fresh herbs, finely chopped (basil, chives, or parsley)

Directions:

1. Pre-heat oven to 450 °F (230 °C).

2. In a large bowl, coat the potatoes with a dash of olive oil, salt, and pepper to taste. Place the potatoes, skin side up, on a large baking pan. Roast for 10 minutes.

3. Tear off 4 sheets of foil, each approximately 12" long. Divide the tomatoes and place one portion in the middle of each sheet. Add a piece of fish seasoned with salt and pepper, and top with lemon and a tsp. olive oil. Lift the corners of the foil and pinch the edges together tightly to form envelopes.

4. Arrange the en papillote envelopes on top of the potatoes and bake for approximately 15 minutes more.

5. Remove the envelopes and potatoes from oven. Crack open the foil envelopes and allow to rest for 10 minutes.

6. Top the potatoes with the fish fillets and tomatoes. Drizzle with the cooking juices left in the foil packets and garnish with chopped herbs.

SEAFOOD & FISH

JAPANESE-STYLE SEA BASS

Miso, or fermented soy bean paste, is a traditional Japanese seasoning rich in umami flavor.

COOKING TIME: 35 MINUTES | SERVINGS: 4

Ingredients:

- 1/3 cup miso paste
- 2 lemons, zested and juiced
- 4 black sea bass fillets with skin, 1" thick (substitute red snapper or halibut if desired)
- 1 lb. kale, chopped
- 1 lb. shiitake mushrooms, thickly sliced

Directions:

1. Pre-heat oven to 450 °F (230 °C). Line a baking sheet with parchment paper.

2. Prepare the sauce by beating the miso paste, a dash of olive oil, lemon juice, zest, salt, and pepper together. Coat the fish with the sauce.

3. Knead and bruise the kale with your hands to soften it before tossing it in with the mushrooms, several tbsp. olive oil, as well as salt and pepper to taste. Place the mixture on the baking sheet and flatten evenly. Put the mixture in the oven until the kale begins to get crispy (approx. 10 minutes).

4. Take the kale out of the oven and use a spatula to break up the mixture. Then, flatten the broken kale into an even bed once again. Arrange the fish fillets on top and return to the oven for another 12-15 minutes.

5. Serve with rice, lemon wedges, and soy sauce.

SEAFOOD & FISH

SRIRACHA SHRIMP PATTIES

Serve these patties with a side salad, or pop them on a bun for a gourmet burger.

COOKING TIME: 25 MINUTES | SERVINGS: 3

Ingredients:

- 2 lbs. frozen shrimp, thawed
- ½ cup mayonnaise
- ½ cup maple syrup
- 2 tsp. sriracha sauce
- 2 tbsp. lime juice

Directions:

1. Make sure that the shrimp have all been properly cleaned, with both the upper and lower intestines removed. Toss the cleaned shrimp into a food processor, along with the mayonnaise, and salt and pepper to taste. Blend until the mixture resembles lumpy pancake batter.

2. Heat a dash of oil in a large non-stick skillet over a medium to high heat. Once it's very hot, add the shrimp (Note: it's best to use your hands to form the patties). Fry the patties for 3 minutes, or until browned on the bottom, then turn and cook for another 2 minutes. (Note: cook the patties in several batches rather than crowding the pan.)

3. Remove the patties to a warmed dish and quickly clean the pan with a paper towel before using it to heat the sriracha sauce, lime juice, and maple syrup. Stir occasionally, until the sauce is thick and gooey. Drizzle this sauce over the patties before serving.

SEAFOOD & FISH

SAUCY SEAFOOD TACOS

Shrimp cooks in mere minutes, making this dish perfect for a light yet satisfying weeknight dinner.

COOKING TIME: 25 MINUTES | SERVINGS: 3

Ingredients:

- 1 lb. shrimp, thawed
- 2 tbsp. taco seasoning powder
- 1 cup salsa rojo
- 2 cups coleslaw
- 6 taco shells

Directions:

1. Ensure that all the shrimp have been properly cleaned and their intestines removed before tossing them in with a tsp. olive oil, half the taco seasoning, and a dusting of cornflour. Allow the shrimp to marinate for a few minutes.

2. Heat a tbsp. oil in a large non-stick skillet and fry the marinated shrimp in two batches for 4 minutes each.

3. Transfer the shrimp to a plate.

4. Add ½ cup water to the pan and cook for 1 minute while scraping the caked-on seasoning off the bottom. Add the salsa and continue to simmer for 5 minutes, or until about half the liquid has evaporated.

5. Chop the shrimp and return to the pan. Stir to combine the shrimp with the sauce.

6. Heat the taco shells by microwaving them and then assemble your tacos with the shrimp before serving.

SEAFOOD & FISH

EASY OVEN-BAKED SALMON

Salmon doesn't need much to make it pop; a little garlic, some acidity, and a sprinkling of herbs is all you need to add.

COOKING TIME: 35 MINUTES | SERVINGS: 6

INGREDIENTS:

- 2 tbsp. crushed garlic (about 6 cloves)
- 4 tbsp. olive oil
- 6 thick salmon fillets
- 4 lemons
- ½ oz. fresh parsley

DIRECTIONS:

1. Pre-heat oven to 350 °F (175 °C).

2. Juice the lemons and finely chop the parsley (Note: you should get about 2/3 and ¼ cups, respectively). Heat a spoonful of oil in a small saucepan and cook the garlic for 1 minute to release its flavor.

3. Mix the lemon juice, parsley, garlic, and olive oil together, along with some salt and pepper to taste.

4. Line a baking pan with parchment paper and space the salmon fillets evenly. Drizzle the fillets with the sauce.

5. Bake for 25-30 minutes, until salmon is firm and flaky.

SEAFOOD & FISH

BROILED LOBSTER TAILS

Cooking an expensive ingredient for the first time can be a little intimidating. But never fear! With lobster, the secret is mostly just to not mess too much with its natural flavor.

COOKING TIME: 30 MINUTES | SERVINGS: 6

Ingredients:

- 6 lobster tails, fresh or frozen and thawed
- ¾ cup olive oil
- ½ oz. fresh chives
- 3 cloves garlic

Directions:

1. Peel the garlic and mince along with the chives.

2. Open the top of the shell using a sturdy pair of kitchen scissors (Note: don't cut off the fin at the back). Pry the meat away from the shell using your thumb. Peel the meat out without tearing off the fin and place the meat on top of the shell for a nice presentation.

3. Whisk the oil, garlic, herbs, salt, and pepper together.

4. Score the lobster meat approximately ½" deep from front to back using a paring knife. Pour over the marinade and leave in the fridge for about half an hour.

5. Heat your barbecue to medium and place the lobster, shell base down, on the grill. Close the lid and cook for 10-12 minutes (Note: your lobsters are done when their centers are white and no longer translucent).

SEAFOOD & FISH

FISH WITH LATIN-STYLE RICE

A small number of people really hate the taste of cilantro, so ask before preparing this dish for guests.

COOKING TIME: 30 MINUTES | SERVINGS: 4

Ingredients:

- 6 oz. fresh cilantro
- 2 tbsp. apple cider vinegar
- 2 cloves garlic
- 1 cup uncooked rice
- 4 fish fillets, 1" thick and skinned (cod, haddock, black sea bass, hake, or pollack)

Directions:

1. Pre-heat oven to 425 °F (220 °C). Move the wire rack to the middle slot.

2. Peel and crush the garlic. Roughly chop the cilantro (Note: don't use the tougher stems).

3. Take out your food processor and process the cilantro, garlic, vinegar, salt, and pepper into a coarse paste. Spoon the paste into a bowl and combine with several tbsp. olive oil to turn it into a sauce.

4. Fill a medium pot with water, add 1 tsp. salt, and place on medium heat. Once boiling, add rice and cook for 12 minutes, or until the rice is tender. Drain the rice in a colander or sieve, return to the pot, and toss with ¼ cup of the sauce.

5. Season the fish with salt and pepper to taste. Place a wide cast-iron pan with a non-plastic handle over high heat. Once hot, add the fillets to sear for approximately 2 minutes.

6. Turn the fish and move the pan to the oven. Bake for another 8 minutes, or until the fish is cooked through. Serve on the seasoned rice with a splash of sauce on top.

SEAFOOD & FISH

ITALIAN RICE WITH SHRIMP

Using the shells to make a seafood stock is a restaurant trick that, while something of a chore, is well worth it.

COOKING TIME: 55 MINUTES | SERVINGS: 4

Ingredients:

- 1 lb. fresh shrimp
- 4 shallots
- 6 cloves garlic
- 1½ cups uncooked risotto rice
- 1 tsp. minced chipotle chilis in adobo sauce

Directions:

1. Peel and crush the garlic and chop the shallots. Shell and clean the shrimp (Note: watching a YouTube video on the subject may help if you've never done this before) and then chop them into chunks.

2. Place a wide, deep pot on high heat. Once hot, add a dash of olive oil and the shrimp shells. Cook for approximately 3 minutes, or until the shells are slightly charred. Stir frequently.

3. Add 5½ cups water and a large pinch of salt. Use a spatula to scrape up the brown fond sticking to the bottom to release its flavor. Simmer on low for 5 minutes, then pour through a sieve to remove the shells. Pour back into the pot and keep hot.

4. Melt 3 tbsp. butter in a crockpot or saucepan. Cook the shallots on medium heat until translucent. Add garlic and fry for half a minute, stirring continuously. Add in the dry rice and stir to coat with butter. Cook the rice mixture for approximately 3 minutes.

5. Ladle in 4 cups of the shrimp stock with the rice and simmer until slightly tender (approx. 16-19 minutes).

6. Pour in another cup of shrimp stock, stirring continually, until most of the stock has been absorbed and the rice achieves a smooth texture (approx. 5 minutes).

7. Remove the rice mixture from the hob and mix in the chopped shrimp. Within 5 minutes, the heat from the rice would have cooked the shrimp so that they are firm.

8. Add more stock if the rice is too dry. Add salt and pepper to taste.

9. Heat 3 tbsp. butter, the minced chilis, and 3 tbsp. of the chili jar's sauce in a small saucepan or microwave. Splash over each serving, or serve on the side.

SEAFOOD & FISH

SALMON FISHCAKES

Using canned salmon is usually much more convenient and still allows you to enjoy this oily fish's flavor.

COOKING TIME: 25 MINUTES | SERVINGS: 3

Ingredients:

- 2 lbs. salmon, canned, fresh, or frozen and thawed
- 2/3 cup mayonnaise
- 2 tsp. mustard powder
- ¾ cup almond flour
- 1 green onion, chopped
- Tartar sauce, for serving

Directions:

1. If using whole salmon fillets, peel off the skin with the help of a sharp knife and slice the fillets into 1" cubes.

2. Wet the almond flour with a few teaspoons water until it just starts to form a paste. Leave the paste for 3 minutes to absorb the moisture completely.

3. Add all the ingredients except the tartar sauce to a food processor, along with salt and pepper to taste. Blend the ingredients until creamy, with a few shreds of fish remaining.

4. Place a wide skillet on high heat. Once hot, add a few spoonful's of oil and use your hands to form the fishcakes. Fry the cakes until browned, then turn to cook through (approx. 8 minutes in total).

5. Serve with lemon wedges or tartar sauce on the side.

BEEF, LAMB & PORK

BEEF, LAMB & PORK

HAWAIIAN BEEF WRAPS

Try this instead of boring sandwiches if you have some leftover beef lying around.

COOKING TIME: 15 MINUTES | SERVINGS: 4

Ingredients:

- 8 oz. tub cream cheese
- 4 soft tortillas
- 4 cups fresh spinach
- ¾ lb. thinly sliced roast beef
- 1 cup fresh fruit (mango, pineapple, or a mixture)

Directions:

1. Coat the tortillas with cream cheese, leaving the fringe dry. Add the other ingredients, wrap, and serve.

BEEF, LAMB & PORK

BBQ PULLED BEEF SANDWICHES

Slow cookers are miracle workers. Although you have to start this dish well in advance, the actual work involved is minimal.

COOKING TIME: 8 HOURS | SERVINGS: 8

INGREDIENTS:

- 3 lbs. beef chuck, deboned
- 1¼ oz. hot spice mix
- ½ cup BBQ sauce
- 8 unbaked rolls
- 8 slices cheese

DIRECTIONS:

1. Slice the meat into three equal pieces before coating with the spices and sauce. Place the meat in a crockpot on low heat for 8-10 hours.

2. Cook the rolls according to the instructions on the packaging.

3. Remove the meat and pull it apart into slivers using two forks. Place the meat back into the crockpot to heat.

4. Assemble the sandwiches.

BEEF, LAMB & PORK

ONE-PAN BEEF DINNER

Once in a while, all of us have days when we just don't have the energy to cook anything complicated. Don't order pizza; try this simple, filling dish instead.

COOKING TIME: 45 MINUTES | SERVINGS: 6

Ingredients:

- 1 lb. lean mince, beef or lamb
- 2 lbs. potatoes
- 2 cups corn kernels
- 1 onion
- 10¾ oz. can concentrated cream of mushroom soup

Directions:

1. Chop the onion and peel the potatoes; cut everything into ½" cubes.

2. Break the mince into small pieces and place in a large pan with a lid. Add the vegetables in a layer on top of the meat, along with salt and pepper to taste. Pour over the soup.

3. Place the lid on the pan and cook on medium for 10 minutes.

4. Lower the heat and simmer for another 30 minutes, or until you can easily pierce the potatoes with a fork.

BEEF, LAMB & PORK

PEPPERS STUFFED WITH RICE AND BEEF

Served with all the ingredients jumbled up together, this dish would be unremarkable. Taking a few minutes to stuff the peppers makes all the difference when it comes to presentation.

COOKING TIME: 1 HOUR | SERVINGS: 8

Ingredients:

- 8 green bell peppers of roughly equal size and shape
- 1 lb. lean mince, beef or lamb
- 14½ oz. can tomatoes, diced
- 5½ oz. seasoned Mexican rice mix
- 2 cups cheese, grated

Directions:

1. Set oven to 375 °F (190 °C) and leave to heat up while you prepare the ingredients.

2. Use a paring knife to cut around the stems of the peppers. Pull out the seeds and pith, being careful not to tear the flesh.

3. Bring a pot of water to the boil and add the peppers. Blanche the peppers for approximately 4 minutes, then rinse them under the tap to keep them from overcooking.

4. Cook the mince in a wide pan on medium heat until browned. Pour off the excess fat, then add the tomatoes, rice, and 1½ cups of water. Put on the lid and simmer for 8 minutes, until the rice is tender and fluffy.

5. Stuff each pepper with the rice-and-mince mixture. Top with cheese.

6. Arrange the peppers on a lined baking tray, with additional rice over and around them. Cover with tinfoil and bake for 25 minutes.

7. Spread the rest of the cheese over the top and return to the oven, uncovered, for another 5-10 minutes.

Tip: Add a can of black beans, drained and rinsed, to stretch this recipe (and make it a little healthier for your heart).

BEEF, LAMB & PORK

FRIED RICE WITH KIMCHI

Kimchi, or cabbage fermented with garlic, ginger, and red pepper, is to Korean cuisine what French fries are to American. It can be eaten raw, but adds a deliciously subtle flavor when cooked with other ingredients.

COOKING TIME: 30 MINUTES | SERVINGS: 4

Ingredients:

- 1 lb. uncooked ham roast
- 1¼ cups kimchi
- 3 tbsp. gochujang paste
- 6 spring onions
- 4 cups cooked, refrigerated rice

Directions:

1. Slice the ham into small (approx. ¼") cubes. Roughly chop the kimchi into pieces of about 1" wide. Separate the green leaves and white stems of the spring onions and slice both into ribbons, lengthwise.

2. Heat a dash of oil in a large pan or wok. Stir-fry the ham over high heat until its cooked through (approx. 7 minutes).

3. Add the other ingredients, except for the sliced spring onions, to the wok. Throw in 2 tbsp. water and ½ a cup of the kimchi brine, with salt and pepper to taste. Stir gently until all the ingredients are evenly distributed.

4. Use your spatula to compact the rice against the pan or wok's base. Put on the lid and leave the rice alone for 2 minutes. Remove the lid, reduce the heat, and cook for another 5 minutes. Ideally, the bottom of the rice will get slightly brown and crispy.

5. Transfer to bowls, garnish with spring onions, and serve.

BEEF, LAMB & PORK

PORK CHOPS WITH TANGY STRING BEANS

Pork chops are a perennial favorite, but you don't need to serve them the same way every time.

COOKING TIME: 35 MINUTES | SERVINGS: 4

Ingredients:

- 2 tbsp. fresh chives
- 1 lemon
- 4 pork chops
- 1 lb. string beans
- 1 tbsp. horseradish paste

Directions:

1. Zest the lemon to produce ½ tsp., then slice into wedges. Finely chop the chives and cut the ends off the beans.

2. Use a fork to squish the chives, zest, and salt and pepper to taste into 2 oz. of butter until well mixed.

3. Use kitchen scissors to snip through the fat around each pork chop so it doesn't curl up while cooking. Season the chops with salt and pepper.

4. Heat a wide, heavy-bottomed pan over a high heat. Add a dash of oil and the pork chops. Turn frequently until fully cooked and nicely colored (approx. 12 minutes, depending on thickness).

5. Remove the pork chops and top with a pat of the seasoned butter. Cover with foil and set to one side.

6. Add a bit more oil to the pan, if needed, and stir-fry the string beans with a little salt and pepper for approximately 4 minutes. Add ¼ cup of water and scrape the brown crust off the bottom. Put the lid on the pan and simmer until the beans turn a lighter shade of green. Remove the lid and allow most of the liquid to simmer away.

7. Toss the beans in the pan with the rest of the butter and horseradish paste. Continue to cook until beans are soft but still somewhat crunchy.

8. Serve the pork chops with beans and lemon wedges on the side.

BEEF, LAMB & PORK

GRILLED INDIAN ADANA KABOBS

Cool mint and yogurt balance out the heat of the tikka masala spices.

COOKING TIME: 30 MINUTES | SERVINGS: 1

Ingredients:

- 1½ pounds lean mince, beef or lamb
- ½ cup tikka masala sauce
- ½ oz. fresh mint
- 1½ cups plain yogurt
- 1 each yellow, green, and red sweet peppers

Directions:

1. Mince the herbs and core the peppers. Slice the peppers into wide strips and season.

2. If using wooden or bamboo skewers, soak them in water for half an hour to prevent splinters.

3. Start your grill approximately 15 minutes before you're ready to begin cooking so it can reach the proper temperature.

4. Using your fingers, mix the mince with all but 2 tbsp. of the tikka masala sauce, half the mint, and salt and pepper to taste. Cover each skewer with a layer of beef, trying to produce cylinders of equal thickness. Work the meat as little as possible to keep it from becoming too chewy. Put the kabobs in the refrigerator for half an hour so they'll keep their shape during cooking.

5. Mix the yogurt with the rest of the mint, sauce, and salt and pepper to taste.

6. Baste the kabobs and sweet pepper slices with a little oil and place on the grill. Roast until the skin of the peppers is slightly charred and the meat is cooked through. Serve with the yogurt sauce.

MEDITERRANEAN LAMB CHOPS

Tahini, a paste made from toasted sesame seeds, is a delicious condiment used throughout the Middle East.

COOKING TIME: 30 MINUTES | SERVINGS: 4

INGREDIENTS:

- 2 lbs. lamb chops
- ½ cup tahini paste
- 2 cloves garlic
- 1 lemon, zested and juiced
- 4 oz. fresh parsley
- Olive oil. For serving

DIRECTIONS:

1. Season the lamb chops with salt, pepper, and whatever other spices catch your eye (Note: smoked paprika is a good choice). Finely chop the parsley, and peel and crush the garlic.

2. Add the garlic to the lemon juice. Marinate for approximately 5 minutes, then whisk with the tahini, 1/3 cup water, half the chopped parsley, and salt and pepper to taste. Keep whisking until you see the mixture becomes smooth and a little runny. Add water as needed.

3. Pat the lamb chops dry using paper towels and season with salt and pepper while heating a large, heavy-bottomed skillet over high heat. Cook only a few chops at a time – the idea is to keep the pan very hot so the chops will form a crispy crust on the outside (approx. 2-3 minutes a side).

4. Smear a little of the tahini sauce on each plate, arrange a couple of chops around it, and garnish with lemon zest, more parsley, a dollop of sauce, and a few drops of olive oil.

CORNED BEEF CALZONES

Modeled on the famous Reuben sandwich, these pizza pockets combine tangy and savory flavors.

COOKING TIME: 30 MINUTES | SERVINGS: 4

Ingredients:

- 14 oz. raw pizza dough
- 4 oz. Swiss cheese, sliced
- 1 cup pickled or fermented cabbage
- ½ lb. deli corned beef, sliced
- Russian salad dressing

Directions:

1. Allow oven to reach 400 °F (200 °C) while you prepare the rest of the ingredients.

2. Sprinkle a generous amount of flour on a clean, dry countertop. Roll out the pizza dough into a rectangle (approx. 12" long on each side) and then divide it into four equal pieces.

3. Place one quarter of the fillings on each dough piece, leaving ½" of the dough bare around the rim. Fold over diagonally and pinch the edges closed.

4. Line a baking pan with parchment paper and evenly space the calzones on it. Bake for 15-18 minutes, or until the crust is crispy and golden. Drizzle with Russian dressing before serving.

CHEESY BEEF BURRITOS

A few minutes in the oven can take your burritos from ordinary to amazing, especially where presentation is concerned.

COOKING TIME: 30 MINUTES | SERVINGS: 4

Ingredients:

- 1 can mild taco or enchilada sauce
- ¾ cup green salsa
- 1 lb. lean mince, beef
- 4 tortilla wraps
- 1½ cups cheese, grated

Directions:

1. Pre-heat oven to 375 °F (190 °C).

2. Stir enchilada sauce and salsa together.

3. Place a saucepan on medium heat, add the beef in small chunks, and brown. When done, remove the meat from the heat and toss with ½ cup of the sauce.

4. Place one quarter of the cooked mince in a line along the middle of each tortilla. Sprinkle a small handful of cheese over this meat. Roll the tortilla into a tube.

5. Line up the burritos in an oven-safe tray lined with tinfoil or parchment paper. Top with the rest of the sauce and cheese. Bake for 10-15 minutes, or until the cheese is runny.

BEEF, LAMB & PORK

BRAISED BEEF WITH CRANBERRY GRAVY

This recipe serves a crowd without having to spend all that much time in the kitchen.

COOKING TIME: 6 HOURS | SERVINGS: 12

Ingredients:

- 1 onion
- 3 lbs. uncooked beef roast (chuck or brisket)
- 14 oz. can cranberry sauce
- ½ cup cranberry juice concentrate
- 2 tbsp. cornstarch

Directions:

1. Cut the meat in half to fit a large crockpot. Slice up the onion. Whisk together the cranberry sauce and juice.

2. Lay the onion pieces on the bottom of the crockpot, with the roast on top of the onion. Cover with the cranberry mixture.

3. Cook on low for approximately 5½ hours. Remove the roast to a plate and cover loosely with foil to let it rest.

4. Make a gravy – after cooling the roast, pour the cooking liquid from the crockpot through a sieve to remove solids and congealed fat. Heat the liquid in a small pot.

5. Whisk the cornstarch with ¼ cold water and then stir it into juices in the pot. Cook until thickened.

6. Carve the roast against the grain before serving.

BEEF, LAMB & PORK

TOASTED TORTILLAS WITH BEANS

This snack combines crunchy and smooth textures and can be ready in minutes.

COOKING TIME: 20 MINUTES | SERVINGS: 4

INGREDIENTS:

- 15 oz. can black beans
- 16 oz. can re-fried pinto beans
- ½ lb. very lean mince, beef or lamb
- 10 oz. can diced tomatoes in juice
- 8 corn tostadas or poppadoms

DIRECTIONS:

1. Warm the re-fried beans in the microwave, mash with a fork if necessary.

2. Drain and rinse the black beans.

3. Brown the beef in a pan over medium heat. Add the tomatoes and simmer for approximately 8 minutes to concentrate. Add in the black beans.

4. Coat the crispy tortilla shells with the re-fried bean paste. Top with the tomato, black beans, and beef filling.

5. Serve with assorted garnishes (e.g., grated cheese, salsa, avocado slices, and sour cream).

BEEF, LAMB & PORK

SLIGHTLY SPICY ROAST PORK

Using the same baking dish for both the meat and the sides saves on the amount of washing up you'll have to do later.

COOKING TIME: 40 MINUTES | SERVINGS: 4

Ingredients:

- 1 jalapeño pepper
- ¼ cup hoisin sauce
- 2 pork tenderloins
- 1 lb. asparagus stems
- 8 green onions
- Olive oil

Directions:

1. Pre-heat oven to 450 °F (230 °C).

2. Remove the stem and seeds from the jalapeño before chopping it up very finely. In a small bowl, mash the chili with 4 tbsp. butter and 1 tbsp. hoisin sauce.

3. Remove the silver-skin membrane from the pork using a sharp knife. Season, place in a lined baking dish, and baste with the remaining hoisin sauce.

4. Bake for approximately 22 minutes, or until only slightly pink in the middle. Remove and cover with tinfoil to keep the pork warm.

5. Cut off the woody asparagus stems and slice the green onions into 3" lengths. Toss the vegetables with salt and pepper to taste, along with enough olive oil to cover. Place in one layer in baking dish and bake for 8-10 minutes.

6. Serve the pork, sliced into ½" slices, on a bed of the vegetables with seasoned butter on the side.

BREADED PORK CUTLETS WITH HERBS

Za'ater is a classic Middle Eastern herb mix, while herbes de provence is French. Either can help you see pork in a new light.

COOKING TIME: 35 MINUTES | SERVINGS: 4

INGREDIENTS:

- 2 small acorn squashes
- 12-16 oz. pork tenderloin
- 1 cup plain yogurt
- 1¼ cups breadcrumbs
- 3 tbsp. herbes de provence or za'atar mix

DIRECTIONS:

1. Pre-heat oven to 475 °F (245 °C).

2. Slice the squashes in half from stem to base, remove the seeds, and cut into slices of about 1½" thick. Coat with 2 tbsp. olive oil, with salt and pepper to taste.

3. Trim the silver-skin off the pork and cut into 4 portions.

4. Place the squash slices on a baking tin with the skin facing up. Bake for about 25 minutes, or until the pork is tender.

5. Place the pork portions between two sheets of saran wrap. Use a rolling pin or kitchen mallet to flatten them along the grain until they're about ¼" thick.

6. Combine half the yogurt, ¼ cup water, salt, and pepper in a wide bowl. Take another bowl and mix the herbs, breadcrumbs, and a pinch each of salt and pepper.

7. Dip the pork cutlets into the yogurt and then press each cutlet down on the breadcrumbs to coat.

8. Place a wide, heavy-bottomed frying pan on high heat. Add 1 cup oil and let it get very hot. Cook the cutlets, two at a time, until the breading is nicely browned and the meat is cooked through (approx. 2-3 minutes per side). Drain on paper towels when done.

9. Serve the pork and vegetables with the rest of the yogurt and additional the herb mix on the side.

COMFORT FOOD

CRAZY WEEKDAY BEEF-AND-PASTA SOUP

Made from ingredients you may well have in your pantry and freezer, this is the perfect recipe for those nights when relaxing is the only thing on your mind.

COOKING TIME: 25 MINUTES | SERVINGS: 5

INGREDIENTS:

- 1 lb. lean mince, beef
- 2 cups assorted frozen vegetables
- 14½ oz. can diced tomatoes in juice
- 2 cups beef stock
- ½ cup uncooked farfalle, macaroni, fusilli, or other short-cut pasta

DIRECTIONS:

1. Heat a large skillet and brown the beef over medium heat.

2. Pour off any excess grease and then add the other ingredients – all except for the pasta – and return to the stove. Season to taste with salt, pepper, and any other herbs and spices you like.

3. Once boiling, add the pasta, put the lid on the skillet, and simmer for approximately 10 minutes until the vegetables and pasta are cooked.

COMFORT FOOD

FEEL-GOOD SLIDERS

This dish can be served as an appetizer or as a full meal. Given a choice of toppings, kids love to assemble their own.

COOKING TIME: 25 MINUTES | SERVINGS: 8

INGREDIENTS:

- 1 lb. lean mince, beef
- 1 lb. pork sausage meat
- 1 cup BBQ sauce
- 16 slider buns
- Garnishes of your choice (lettuce leaves, pickle slices, sliced tomatoes, red onion, etc.)

DIRECTIONS:

1. Wet your hands and combine the mince and pork (Note: don't overwork the meat or your patties will be tough). Form the mixed meat into 16 meatballs, then press them down on a cutting board until each is around a ½" thick.

2. Cook the patties in a skillet or on a grill for approximately 3½ minutes per side. Baste with BBQ sauce when they're almost done.

3. Halve the rolls and serve with the rest of the barbecue sauce and whatever other toppings you have on hand.

Tip: It's not a bad idea to make extra patties for next time. Arrange them on a plate or dish lined with wax paper and freeze. Once frozen, place the patties in a sealed Tupperware container or Ziplock bag.

COMFORT FOOD

WISCONSIN BEER BRATS

Poaching the bratwurst in beer not only seasons the sausage but ensures that it will never be undercooked after grilling.

COOKING TIME: 25 MINUTES | SERVINGS: 8

INGREDIENTS:

- 8 bratwurst or kielbasa, uncooked
- 36 oz. cans beer
- 1 large onion
- 2 tbsp. fennel seed
- 8 hot dog buns

DIRECTIONS:

1. Empty the cans of beer into a crockpot. Toss in the sausage, sliced onion, and fennel seed. Simmer until the meat is cooked (approx. 10 minutes). Remove the sausage.

2. Grill the sausage with the barbecue's lid closed on moderate heat for approximately 8 minutes. Serve on buns with grated cheese, sauces, or chopped fresh herbs.

COMFORT FOOD

(NEARLY) INSTANT GUMBO

Purists will say that gumbo needs to be simmered for at least 3 hours before attaining the right flavor and texture. They may be right, but this busy person's adaptation comes close enough.

COOKING TIME: 20 MINUTES | SERVINGS: 6

INGREDIENTS:

- 3 Italian, turkey, or bratwurst sausages
- 14½ oz. can diced tomatoes in juice
- 1¾ cups chicken stock
- 1 cup uncooked instant rice
- 2 cups assorted vegetables (corn kernels, chopped onion, sweet pepper, or mixed frozen vegetables

DIRECTIONS:

1. Cook the sausages in a large, wide pot until firm and no longer pink in the middle. Remove, slice, and pour off excess grease.

2. Add vegetables and cook for approximately 4 minutes, or until tender.

3. Place the tomatoes, stock, and half a cup of water in the pot and turn up the heat. Once boiling, stir in the instant rice, put on the lid, and turn off the stove. Let the gumbo rest for 5 minutes before serving.

COMFORT FOOD

CREAMY SHRIMP AND BROCCOLI PASTA

Being short of time is no excuse for not getting some vegetables in your diet.

COOKING TIME: 10 MINUTES | SERVINGS: 4

INGREDIENTS:

- 32 oz. boxes frozen fettuccine alfredo
- 2 cups baby broccoli, chopped
- 22 oz. frozen cooked shrimp
- Parmesan cheese to serve

DIRECTIONS:

1. Set a large pot on medium heat. Add the broccoli and shrimp, along with the amount of water recommended on the pasta's packaging.

2. Put the lid on the pot and cook for 2 minutes, then mix thoroughly.

3. Return the lid and simmer on low heat until all ingredients are hot enough to serve (approx. 5 minutes).

4. Spoon into bowls and dust with the parmesan cheese.

KEBAB MEAT IN PITA POCKETS

Greece's most famous contribution to the world of fast food, gyros are a light, healthy meal that can be prepared in minutes.

COOKING TIME: 15 MINUTES | SERVINGS: 2

Ingredients:

- 8 oz. doner kebab or gyro meat
- ¼ red onion
- 2 tomatoes
- 2 pita bread pockets
- ½ cup tzatziki sauce

Directions:

1. If raw, cook the meat in a large non-stick skillet until well done (approx. 10 minutes). Stir occasionally.

2. Slice the onion thinly and the tomatoes a little more coarsely.

3. Stuff the pitas, spooning the tzatziki over the opening.

STIR-FRIED BLACK BEAN SAUCE CHICKEN

Aside from having the local takeout place's phone number, Chinese cuisine is kind of a mystery to most people. One of its secrets is that meat is rarely cooked without being marinated, even if only for a few minutes.

COOKING TIME: 35 MINUTES | SERVINGS: 4

INGREDIENTS:

- 1½ lbs. chicken thighs, skinless and deboned
- 6 green onions
- 1/3 cup black bean sauce
- 2 tbsp. soy sauce
- 1 lb. assorted frozen vegetables, thawed

DIRECTIONS:

1. Slice the chicken crosswise into ¼" strips. Cut the green leaves of the scallions into 1" sections and chop the white stems into thin rounds.

2. Prepare the marinade by combining ¼ cup water and the black bean and soy sauces in a small bowl. Toss the chicken with 3 tbsp. of this mixture and let the flavors infuse for 10 minutes.

3. Heat a wok or large, heavy-bottomed pan over high heat. Add a dash of oil and stir-fry the chicken in two batches. Transfer to a plate when done.

4. Wipe out the pan with some paper towels before returning to the heat. Once it's hot again, sear the thawed vegetables for half a minute in a little oil. Splash in 2 tbsp. water and put on the lid. Turn down the heat and cook for another 2 minutes, or until the vegetables are done but still crisp.

5. Use a spatula to scrape the vegetables to the edges of the pan. Place the chopped whites of the onion in the center and cook for 1 minute, bruising the onions to release their flavor.

6. Return the chicken to the pan and mix. Add the remaining black bean sauce mixture and stir vigorously until all ingredients are coated. Add the green parts of the scallions and serve.

COMFORT FOOD

STRIP STEAKS WITH SAUTEED POTATOES

It's possible to pan-fry potatoes from raw, but partially cooking them in the microwave saves a lot of time and helps them to better soak up the meat's cooking juices.

COOKING TIME: 50 MINUTES | SERVINGS: 4

INGREDIENTS:

- 1½ lbs. Yukon gold, Charlotte, or russet potatoes
- 2 ½-lb. strip steaks
- ½ cup basil pesto

DIRECTIONS:

1. There's no need to peel the potatoes, just cut them into wedges of about 1" across. Then, toss the potatoes with 1 tbsp. olive oil, with salt and pepper to taste before placing them in a covered bowl and microwaving on high for 10 minutes.

2. Slice each steak in two. Dry the steak pieces' surface with paper towels to ensure that they sear properly. Season with salt and pepper.

3. Heat a dash of oil in a large, heavy-bottomed pan over high heat. Pan-fry the steaks, turning every 2 minutes or so. Steaks 1-1½" thick should take approximately 10-12 minutes to reach medium-rare. Once cooked, remove the steaks from the pan and cover with tinfoil to keep them warm.

4. Heat 4 tbsp. oil in the same pan. Sauté the potatoes in two batches for 8-12 minutes. Stir carefully from time to time. Drain on paper towels when done.

5. Toss the potato wedges with pesto before serving alongside the steaks.

COMFORT FOOD

KALE AND MUSHROOM TAGLIATELLE

Kale gets a bad rap, and to be fair it isn't all that great on its own. But, combined with the right flavors and textures, you'll learn to love this superfood.

COOKING TIME: 25 MINUTES | SERVINGS: 2

INGREDIENTS:

- 8 oz. fettuccine or tagliatelle
- 8 oz. shiitake, porcini, or wild mushrooms
- 5 cloves garlic
- 10 oz. kale
- 1 cup grated parmesan cheese

DIRECTIONS:

1. Heat a large pot of salted water. Slice the mushrooms into chunks, peel and crush the garlic, and shred the kale.

2. Cook the mushrooms in a large, non-stick skillet for approximately 10 minutes with a little oil.

3. Add the kale and garlic, with salt and pepper to taste, and cook for 3 more minutes, until the kale begins to wilt.

4. Cook the pasta for 8 minutes, or according to the packaging's instructions. Drain, but reserve 1 cup of the cooking water.

5. Return the skillet containing the kale and mushrooms to the stove. Mix in the pasta and reserved water. Stir well while cooking, sprinkling on the cheese as you go. Serve hot.

Tip: The reason for adding the pasta's cooking water to the sauce is that the dissolved starch provides a creamy texture and helps the pasta to stick to the sauce.

COMFORT FOOD

ROMAN CARBONARA

In the United States, carbonara sauces are typically made with cream. This is nothing short of heresy in Italy, but…this recipe is closer to the original dish.

COOKING TIME: 25 MINUTES | SERVINGS: 2

Ingredients:

- 3 slices bacon or pancetta
- 8 oz. spaghetti
- ½ cup parmesan cheese, grated
- 4 egg yolks
- ¼ cup fresh parsley, chopped

Directions:

1. Cut the pork into small bits and fry over medium heat until crispy. Fish out the bacon, but don't discard the flavorful grease.

2. Bring a large pot of water to the boil, add 2 tbsp. salt, and cook the spaghetti for approximately 8 minutes until al dente.

3. While the pasta is boiling, whisk together the egg yolks along with the cheese, half the parsley, and salt and pepper to taste.

4. Strain the pasta through a colander, reserving 1 cup of the water. Place the skillet used for frying the bacon back on the heat and add the pasta. Pour over the egg-and-cheese mixture and toss thoroughly. Pour in the reserved water as you stir. (Note: The heat from the pasta should cook the eggs without scrambling them, creating a creamy yet low-fat sauce.)

5. Add the bacon, the rest of the parsley and cheese, as well as more salt and pepper if needed.

CHEWY MEAT CALZONE

Most people like their pizza crust to be crispy, but you can also switch things up by using a softer, fluffier dough.

COOKING TIME: 50 MINUTES | SERVINGS: 6

INGREDIENTS:

- 16 oz. bread dough (French, crescent roll, or sourdough according to preference)
- 1½ lbs. lean mince, beef
- 15 oz. can pizza sauce
- 1 cup cheddar, grated
- 1 cup mozzarella, grated

DIRECTIONS:

1. Set oven to 350 °F (180 °C) and let it heat up while you prepare your ingredients.

2. Place half the dough on a work surface sprinkled with flour. Roll out the dough, if necessary, and press into a baking sheet coated with cooking spray.

3. Brown the beef over medium heat and pour off the excess fat. Cover the dough with the beef.

4. Pour over an even layer of pizza sauce and top with cheese.

5. Roll out the rest of the dough to the same size as the bottom half. Lay this second layer over cheese and pinch closed at the edges.

6. Bake for 30 minutes, or until the top begins to brown.

COMFORT FOOD

ASIAN BEEF NOODLES

In the case of this recipe, the secret really is in the sauce – the other ingredients play supporting roles.

COOKING TIME: 15 MINUTES | SERVINGS: 2

Ingredients:

- 8 oz. steak strips, about ¼" wide
- ½ cup garlic coconut aminos sauce
- 4 scallions
- 5 oz. snow peas or mange tout
- 1 lb. rice noodles

Directions:

1. Toss the steak strips with half the coconut sauce and leave to marinate. Chop the scallions finely, keeping the leaves and white stems separate.

2. Place a wok or large skillet on high heat with a dash of vegetable oil. Once hot, add the peas and stir-fry until slightly charred (approx. 4 minutes).

3. Pat the marinated steak strips dry using a paper towel and add to the skillet along with the white scallions. Add salt and pepper to taste.

4. Cook the noodles according to packaging instructions and keep warm.

5. Once the meat is cooked (approx. 3 minutes), add the noodles to the pan and pour over the remainder of the aminos. Toss well while cooking, and garnish with the green scallions.

Tip: For a low-carb option, replace the rice noodles with shirataki, zucchini, or kelp noodles.

COMFORT FOOD

SIMPLE COWHERD'S PIE

Irish shepherd's pie is traditionally prepared with ground lamb. Our version of this mashed-potato pie uses ground beef instead.

COOKING TIME: 50 MINUTES | SERVINGS: 4

INGREDIENTS:

- 1 lb. mince, beef
- 2 1½ oz. cans concentrated cream of potato soup
- 3 cups frozen peas and carrots, thawed
- 4 cups mashed potatoes

DIRECTIONS:

1. Set oven to 350 °F (180 °C) and allow time for it to get hot.

2. Heat a wide saucepan with some oil and cook the beef until browned. Pour off the excess grease and add the vegetables and condensed soup.

3. Heat the mashed potatoes in the microwave if necessary. Mix in 4 tbsp. butter and a dash of milk.

4. Grease a mid-sized oven-safe ceramic dish and distribute the filling in an even layer. Top with the potatoes.

5. Bake for 30-40 minutes, or until the potatoes start to brown slightly.

VEGETARIAN MAIN COURSES

ZUCCHINI CASSEROLE

Zucchini is cheap, easy to pair with other ingredients, and satisfyingly robust, however it's prepared.

COOKING TIME: 40 MINUTES | SERVINGS: 4

Ingredients:

- 13 oz. zucchini
- 6 oz. mushrooms
- ½ onion
- ½ tsp. dried basil
- ½ cup cheddar, grated

Directions:

1. Turn the oven to 350 °F (180 °C) and let it heat while preparing your ingredients. Grease a large baking pan.

2. Slice the zucchini, mushrooms, and onion into strips. Place the vegetables into a baking dish and mix together with the herbs.

3. Cover with foil and bake for 30 minutes. Remove the foil, top with cheese, and return to the oven for approximately 10 more minutes, or until cheese melts.

VEGETARIAN MAIN COURSES

SUPER-SIMPLE BROCCOLI SOUP

The best part of ramen is sometimes the packet of flavoring. Here the flavoring is used to take the soup from insipid to appetizing.

COOKING TIME: 20 MINUTES | SERVINGS: 7

INGREDIENTS:

- 16 oz. bag frozen broccoli florets
- 6 oz. packages ramen noodles, chicken flavor
- ¼ tsp. garlic powder
- 3 slices cheddar or American cheese

DIRECTIONS:

1. Heat 5 cups of water in a large pot until boiling. Add the broccoli.

2. Once the water boils again, turn down the heat and simmer for 3 minutes, or until the vegetables turn a dark green.

3. Break up the ramen cakes and stir in with the broccoli. Simmer for an additional 3 minutes.

4. Turn off the stove, slice the cheese into strips, and add the rest of the ingredients. Mix well and serve.

Tip: Process the broccoli (or any other soup vegetable for that matter) right in the pot with a stick blender for a smooth texture and attractive appearance.

VEGETARIAN MAIN COURSES

AUTUMN SOUP

Filling and hearty, this is just the thing to get you in a good mood on a cold evening.

COOKING TIME: 20 MINUTES | SERVINGS: 8

INGREDIENTS:

- 15 oz. canned or frozen pumpkin
- 15 oz. can black beans
- 1½ cups frozen corn kernels
- 10 oz. can diced tomatoes and green chilies
- 3½ cups chicken stock

DIRECTIONS:

1. Drain and rinse the beans. If the pumpkin is in solid pieces, finely chop or whiz it in a food processor (after thawing).

2. Toss all the ingredients into a large pot and heat until boiling.

3. Simmer for 15 minutes, or until thickened. Stir occasionally.

4. Serve with hot rolls or cornbread.

Tip: Almost all soups, including this one, freeze well. Make a large batch and save some for a future dinner.

VEGETARIAN MAIN COURSES

SPAGHETTI SQUASH VEGAN "BOLOGNESE"

You don't need to turn vegan to start enjoying aubergine steaks, cauliflower rice, and spaghetti squash. Prepared properly, these alternatives are just as good as the real thing, can be bought pre-made, and make healthier eating a breeze.

COOKING TIME: 45 MINUTES | SERVINGS: 4

Ingredients:

- 1 medium spaghetti squash
- 16 oz. jar vegan bolognese pasta sauce
- Handful fresh parsley, finely chopped

Directions:

1. Set oven to 400 °F (200 °C) and place a sheet of parchment paper on a baking tray. Allow a few minutes for pre-heating.

2. Slice the squash in half from top to bottom and scoop out the seeds. Brush with olive oil on the inside, season with salt and pepper, and bake for 40 minutes, cut side down.

3. Scrape out the inside of the squash with a fork to release strands of flesh resembling spaghetti.

4. Heat the sauce in a large saucepan. Stir in the spaghetti squash to coat and garnish with the parsley.

FUSILLI WITH TOMATO AND SPINACH

Spinach is one of the few vegetables that provide significant quantities of potassium, calcium, magnesium, and iron all in one package. If you're only willing to add one kind of vegetable to your diet, choose spinach.

COOKING TIME: 25 MINUTES | SERVINGS: 4

Ingredients:

- 8 oz. uncooked fusilli
- 10 oz. bag frozen creamed spinach, thawed
- 14½ oz. can diced tomatoes in juice
- 6 tbsp. parmesan cheese, grated

Directions:

1. Bring a large pot of salted water to the boil and cook the fusilli for approximately 10 minutes, or until al dente.

2. Heat the spinach and tomatoes, along with 2/3 of the cheese, stirring occasionally.

3. Drain the pasta and stir in the sauce. Dust with the rest of the cheese to serve.

VEGETARIAN MAIN COURSES

UPGRADED VEGETARIAN ENCHILADA

Surprisingly, some food manufacturers still haven't gotten the memo on how to make vegetarian food appealing. Throwing a few fresh ingredients into the mix can make the average store-bought enchilada a lot more satisfying.

COOKING TIME: 50 MINUTES | SERVINGS: 1

INGREDIENTS:

- 1 frozen black bean & corn enchilada
- 1 tbsp. olive oil
- 1 egg
- 2/3 cup grated cheese
- ½ avocado
- 1 tbsp. sour cream

DIRECTIONS:

1. Set the oven to 350 °F (180 °C), if you have time. Alternatively, use the microwave. (Note: baking results in a crispier enchilada while microwaving leaves it chewier.)

2. Re-heat the enchilada according to instructions on the packaging in either the oven or the microwave.

3. When the enchilada is nearly done, add a little oil to a non-stick pan and fry the egg. Turn the egg once the white is solid and cook until the yolk is firm.

4. Slice the avocado and top the enchilada with this, the cheese, and the sour cream.

SUN-DRIED TOMATO GNOCCHI

Making gnocchi from scratch is something even experienced cooks sometimes have trouble with. Luckily, the store-bought variety is nearly as good and offers an easy alternative.

COOKING TIME: 30 MINUTES | SERVINGS: 4

INGREDIENTS:

- 2 lbs. vacuum-packed or frozen gnocchi
- ½ cup breadcrumbs
- ½ cup sun-dried tomatoes in oil
- 8 cups fresh spinach
- 8 oz. tub ricotta cheese

DIRECTIONS:

1. Remove the stems from the spinach and chop finely. Chop the sun-dried tomatoes into thin strips.

2. Combine the breadcrumbs with 1 tbsp. olive oil and microwave for approximately 3 minutes until toasted, stirring every minute.

3. Boil some salted water in a large saucepan. Throw in the gnocchi and cook according to the packaging instructions. Stir occasionally.

4. Strain the gnocchi through a colander, setting aside 1 cup of the water in the saucepan.

5. Return the saucepan to the stove. Add a ¼ cup of the oil in which the tomatoes were packed. Cook the tomatoes and spinach over moderate heat, stirring continually (approx. 1 minute, or until the spinach wilts).

6. Add the gnocchi and half the starchy water that you set aside earlier. Stir gently but thoroughly.

7. Remove from the heat and stir in the cheese. Add more cooking water to achieve a smooth texture. Season with salt and pepper and serve topped with the breadcrumbs.

SOBA NOODLES WITH JAPANESE SPICES AND ASPARAGUS

This dish contains three fairly exotic ingredients – miso, nori, and shichimi togarashi. None of these ingredients are too hard to find, but may well surprise and delight your dinner guests.

COOKING TIME: 35 MINUTES | SERVINGS: 4

Ingredients:

- ¼ cup miso paste
- 1 tsp. shichimi togarashi spice mix
- 1 lb. asparagus
- 2 sheets nori (dried seaweed)
- 12 oz. soba or rice noodles

Directions:

1. Stir together half the spice mix, miso, 3 tbsp. olive oil, and a ½ cup warm water. Add more water until you get a fluid texture.

2. Trim the hard stems off the asparagus and slice diagonally into 1" pieces. Cut the nori into ribbons (approx. 2" wide) with kitchen shears. Place these ribbons on top of each other and slice into thin strips.

3. Prepare a bowl of ice water and boil plenty of salted water in a large saucepan.

4. Blanch the asparagus in the boiling water for approximately 1½ minutes, or just until they become lighter in color. Scoop them out and place them in the iced water to prevent them from overcooking. After several minutes, dry them with paper towels and toss with the miso mixture.

5. Add the noodles to the saucepan and cook according to the instructions on their packaging. Drain and rinse under running water using a colander. Stir in the miso mixture, along with half the nori. Garnish with the remaining spice mix and nori strips.

CAULIFLOWER AND CHEESE CASSEROLE

Filling and rich, this dish can easily be doubled or tripled to feed more people.

COOKING TIME: 60 MINUTES | SERVINGS: 3

Ingredients:

- ½ large cauliflower
- 1 cup raw cashew nuts
- ¾ cup parmesan, grated
- 1 lemon, zested and juiced
- 12 oz. conchiglie (shell) pasta

Directions:

1. Set oven to 400 °F (200 °C) and leave to heat up. Set a large saucepan of salted water on medium heat.

2. Remove the stem from the cauliflower and cut into rough florets. Cook the cauliflower and cashews in the boiling water for 8-10 minutes, until tender but still slightly crispy.

3. Reserving 1 cup of the water, then strain the cauliflower and nuts through a colander. Place the cauliflower and nuts in a food processor or blender, along with 1 tsp. olive oil, ¼ cup of the cheese, half the lemon juice and all of the zest, half of the reserved water, and salt and pepper to taste. Process until no chunks remain. Add more of the cooking water if needed.

4. Return the saucepan to the stove with more salted water. Cook the pasta until al dente. Drain, once again reserving a cup of the water.

5. Combine the pasta, cauliflower mixture, and about ¾ of the pasta water, adding more if needed. Spoon into a medium-sized roasting pan.

6. Bake, covered with foil, for half an hour. Uncover, sprinkle with the remaining parmesan cheese, and cook for another 5 minutes, or until the cheese starts to brown.

VEGETARIAN MAIN COURSES

BACK-TO-BASICS PIZZA

Instead of loading up these pizzas with heavy toppings, simple ingredients are allowed to shine through.

COOKING TIME: 25 MINUTES | SERVINGS: 3

Ingredients:

- 6½ oz. boxed pizza dough mix
- ½ tsp. dried oregano
- 6 oz. marinara sauce
- 6 oz. mozzarella cheese
- ½ oz. fresh basil

Directions:

1. Pre-heat oven to 425 °F (220 °C).

2. Combine the pizza mix with water and other ingredients according to the instructions on the packaging. Include the oregano and any other herbs you like.

3. Separate the dough into three equal portions if you prefer individual pizzas. Roll out to a thin crust.

4. Dust a baking sheet with flour and bake the dough round(s) for between 8 and 10 minutes.

5. Chop the basil and cut the cheese into thin slices.

6. Coat the crust with a thin layer of tomato sauce, leaving a ½" bare around the edge. Arrange the cheese slices on top (Note: it's not necessary to cover all of the sauce with cheese). Return to the oven for a further 5-10 minutes, or until the cheese has melted and is starting to brown.

7. Top with fresh basil before serving.

BLACK BEAN QUESADILLAS WITH SWEET POTATO MASH

Sweet potato puree is surprisingly easy to make and has a texture that complements many dishes.

COOKING TIME: 30 MINUTES | SERVINGS: 4

INGREDIENTS:

- 2 medium sweet potatoes
- 4x 8" tortillas
- ¾ cup cooked black beans
- ½ cup cheese, grated
- ¾ cup red salsa

DIRECTIONS:

1. Wash the sweet potatoes but do not peel them. Instead, puncture the skin here and there with a fork and then cook in the microwave for approximately 8 minutes on high. Turn the potatoes halfway through cooking (Note: they're done when you can easily stick a fork in them).

2. Drain and rinse the beans. Once the sweet potatoes have cooled, slice each in half and use a spoon to scrape out the flesh. Mash until smooth, seasoning with salt and pepper to taste.

3. Assemble your quesadillas by covering half of each tortilla with sweet potato pulp, followed by the beans and cheese. Fold over the other half to create a semicircle, pressing down gently onto the filling.

4. Place a frying pan on a medium heat, then heat the quesadillas until the tortillas are slightly crisp and the cheese has melted (approx. 2-3 minutes per side). Serve with the salsa on the side.

VEGETARIAN MAIN COURSES

SPICED RED LENTILS WITH CRISPY SHALLOTS

Called "palak dal" in India, this protein-rich dish can be served as a side, or with naan bread as the main course.

COOKING TIME: 45 MINUTES | SERVINGS: 4

Ingredients:

- 10½ oz. dry red lentils
- 1 tbsp. fresh ginger, grated
- 3 onions, thinly sliced
- 1 tbsp. garam masala spice mix
- 6 oz. spinach, deveined and roughly chopped

Directions:

1. Heat a large pot containing 4½ cups of water. Once boiling, add the lentils and water and then reduce the heat to a simmer. Stir occasionally for 18-20 minutes, or until the lentils start to fall apart.

2. Microwave the onions tossed with ½ a cup olive oil on high. Stir occasionally until the onions start turning a rich brown. Continue to heat, half a minute at a time, until they are caramelized.

3. Drain the onions on paper towels and add a pinch of salt and pepper. Combine the spice mix with 3 tbsp. of the onion-infused oil.

4. Beat the lentils until you achieve a grainy paste. Keep simmering until the lentils' texture is similar to oatmeal, or for an additional 5 minutes.

5. Add the spinach and allow to wilt. Add salt and pepper to taste.

6. Serve with spiced oil and caramelized onions on the side.

VEGETARIAN MAIN COURSES

FRIED RICE WITH CHINESE CABBAGE

Cooked rice keeps for about 4 days in the fridge. Don't allow it to spoil; instead, add some vegetables and condiments for a quick, delicious meal.

COOKING TIME: 45 MINUTES | SERVINGS: 4

Ingredients:

- 1½ lbs. bok choi
- 10 cloves garlic
- 4 cups cooked rice
- 2 tbsp. fish sauce
- 1 lime, zested and juiced

Directions:

1. Peel and mince the garlic. Slice the bok choi in half lengthwise, then cut into ½" slices.

2. Place a large frying pan or wok with a lid over high heat with a dash of oil. Once hot, add the bok choi, along with a pinch of salt. Cook for approximately 3 minutes, or until tender and somewhat seared.

3. Add garlic and fry, stirring occasionally, for half a minute, or until it releases its flavor.

4. Add 2 tbsp. oil, the rest of the ingredients, and salt and pepper to taste. Stir, then push the rice down onto the base of the pan. Put on the lid and cook on medium heat for 2 minutes.

5. Remove the lid and cook for another 5 minutes (Notes: the rice should have become slightly crunchy at this point).

6. Break up the rice using a spatula and serve.

RAVIOLI IN BROWNED BUTTER SAUCE

Browned butter sauce isn't difficult to make; it has a nutty flavor and can serve as a base for any kind of herb.

COOKING TIME: 30 MINUTES | SERVINGS: 4

Ingredients:

- ½ cup unsalted butter
- 1 oz. fresh sage
- 20 oz. package fresh, uncooked cheese or mushroom ravioli
- 2 tbsp. lemon juice
- 4 tbsp. grated parmesan cheese

Directions:

1. Chop the sage coarsely and cut the butter into small cubes.

2. Boil the ravioli for 5-7 minutes, or as directed on the packaging. Keep 2 tbsp. of the cooking water separate when draining.

3. Heat the butter in a large, thick-bottomed skillet on medium heat. Stir constantly until the color darkens.

4. Quickly add in the chopped sage and a generous pinch of salt before taking the skillet off the heat.

5. Combine the ravioli, reserved cooking water, lemon juice, and browned butter sauce. Stir gently until the sauce covers all the pasta.

6. Sprinkle with cheese and serve.

VEGETARIAN MAIN COURSES

FARM-STYLE BUTTERNUT SQUASH TART

It's a myth that some people just don't like vegetables – as long as they're prepared like this, that is.

COOKING TIME: 60 MINUTES | SERVINGS: 4

INGREDIENTS:

- 6 oz. tub full-fat cream cheese with herbs
- 6 oz. baby spinach
- 1 lb. butternut squash
- 4 onions
- 1 sheet puff pastry (9" by 9")

DIRECTIONS:

1. Pre-heat oven to 425 °F (220 °C). Place a sheet of wax paper on a baking tray.

2. Make sure that the pastry is properly thawed.

3. Thinly slice the onions. Peel and cube the butternut if using whole squash.

4. Allow the cream cheese to reach room temperature and then whisk together with 2 tbsp. olive oil.

5. Place the spinach and 4 tbsp. water in a large bowl covered with clingfilm (Note: pierce the clingfilm with a fork). Cook in the microwave on high for approximately 4 minutes, or until wilted. Discard all excess liquid using a colander, pressing down on the spinach with a spoon. Roughly chop the spinach.

6. Cook the diced squash in the same bowl as you used for the spinach for approximately 8 minutes, or until soft. Discard any liquid.

7. Heat a large, heavy pan over medium heat, along with a generous dash of oil. Add in the sliced onions, along with salt and pepper to taste, and cook until their color turns to golden brown (approx. 10 minutes). Stir frequently during cooking.

8. Stir the onions, spinach, and squash together until well mixed.

9. Dust a clean, dry working surface with flour and unroll the pastry sheet onto it. Gently roll the pastry out before placing it on the baking tray. Wet ½" along the edges and pinch to form a raised rim.

10. Cover the pastry base, except for the rim, with the cream cheese. Top with the spinach-and-butternut filling.

11. Bake for approximately 25 minutes, or until the crust is nicely browned. Allow to cool on a wire rack for 10 minutes before serving.

SALADS & SIDE DISHES

SALADS & SIDE DISHES

EASY POTATOES AU GRATIN

You've been good all week, so why not forget about your diet for a moment and prepare this sinfully rich side dish?

COOKING TIME: 1¼ HOUR | SERVINGS: 10

INGREDIENTS:

- 3 cups heavy cream
- 1 tsp. minced fresh parsley, thyme, or sage
- 3 lbs. russet potatoes

DIRECTIONS:

1. Set oven to 350 °F (175 °C) and leave to pre-heat while preparing the potatoes. Grease a medium-sized casserole pan.

2. Using a mandolin, slice the potatoes (peeled or unpeeled) very thinly.

3. Stir together the cream, herbs, and salt and pepper to taste. Stack the potatoes loosely in the casserole pan. Top with cream.

4. Bake for approximately 50 minutes, uncovered. The dish is ready when the potatoes have softened and the top begins to turn a golden-brown color.

5. Allow the dish to rest for 10 minutes before serving.

CAPRESE SALAD

Basil, mozzarella, tomatoes: green, white, red – get it? While this salad is meant to resemble the Italian flag, there's nothing stopping you from tossing all the ingredients together instead.

COOKING TIME: 15 MINUTES | SERVINGS: 6

INGREDIENTS:

- 3 regular tomatoes or 15 cherry tomatoes
- 8 oz. mozzarella cheese
- ¼ cup extra-virgin olive oil
- ¼ oz. basil leaves

DIRECTIONS:

1. Slice the cheese and tomatoes very thinly (if using cherry tomatoes, just cut in half). Leave the fresh basil whole or chop, as desired.

2. Intersperse the tomato and cheese slices on a plate, being careful with the presentation. Top with basil, and garnish with olive oil. Add salt and pepper to taste.

SALADS & SIDE DISHES

POPEYE SALAD

We're talking about the cartoon character here, not the restaurant chain. A little bit of egg and bacon add body and protein to this low-calorie dish.

COOKING TIME: 15 MINUTES | SERVINGS: 8

Ingredients:

- 9 oz. spinach
- ½ lb. button mushrooms
- 2 hard-boiled eggs
- 2 tbsp cooked bacon bits
- ½ cup vinaigrette dressing

Directions:

1. Wash and trim the spinach. If using baby spinach, just rinse and snap off the stems.

2. Slice the mushrooms and chop the eggs into small cubes.

3. Toss all the ingredients together except the dressing. Pour over the dressing and toss again just before serving.

SPANISH RICE

This dish goes well with grilled meat. Adjust the spiciness by choosing your preferred brand of salsa roja.

COOKING TIME: 15 MINUTES | SERVINGS: 5

Ingredients:

- 1½ cups red salsa
- 2 cups 1-minute rice
- 1 cup cheese, grated

Directions:

1. Add 1½ cups water and salsa to a pot on medium heat. Once boiling, toss in the rice.

2. Let it rest for 5 minutes while the rice absorbs the moisture and flavor. Mix in the cheese and serve.

SALADS & SIDE DISHES

CARROTS SAUTEED WITH GINGER

Be careful what you pair with this side – it may just end up outshining the main course!

COOKING TIME: 10 MINUTES | SERVINGS: 4

Ingredients:

- 1 lb. baby carrots
- 1 tbsp. butter
- 1½ tsp. fresh ginger, grated
- ½ oz. fresh cilantro

Directions:

1. Slice the baby carrots in half, lengthwise. Mince the cilantro.

2. Heat a large pan over high heat. Once hot, add the butter and carrots. Stir-fry for approximately 5 minutes, until the carrots are soft but still crunchy.

3. Add the ginger and cook, stirring continuously for another minute. Take off the heat and add the cilantro. Season with salt and pepper to taste.

FRUITY BLACK BEANS

A bold take on traditional baked beans, this dish marries sweet and savory flavors.

COOKING TIME: 5 HOURS | SERVINGS: 9

Ingredients:

- 60 oz. cans black beans
- 20 oz. can crushed pineapple
- 1½ tsp. fresh ginger
- 18 oz. bottle BBQ sauce
- ½ lb. cooked bacon bits

Directions:

1. Drain and rinse the beans. Drain the pineapple. Peel and mince the ginger.

2. Add all the ingredients, except the bacon, to a crockpot. Cook on the lowest setting for 5 hours, stirring occasionally.

3. Top with or mix in the bacon when ready to serve.

SALADS & SIDE DISHES

ASIAN SAUTEED ZUCCHINI

The three secrets to stir-frying are: high heat, frequent stirring, and the right choice of flavorings.

COOKING TIME: 20 MINUTES | SERVINGS: 4

Ingredients:

- 1 lb. zucchinis
- 4 tsp. peanut, avocado, or olive oil
- 2 cloves garlic
- 2 tbsp. soy sauce
- ½ tsp. toasted sesame seeds

Directions:

1. Cut the zucchini diagonally into thin slivers (Note: if you prefer to save time and wish to ensure even thickness, use a mandolin). Peel and crush the garlic.

2. Heat the oil in a wok or large frying pan. Stir-fry the zucchini slices until softened.

3. Add the garlic and cook for another 30 seconds, or until the garlic releases its flavor.

4. Remove from heat, toss with the soy sauce, and garnish with sesame seeds to serve.

WARM QUINOA AND BRUSSELS SPROUTS SALAD

Many people think that they hate Brussels sprouts, but that's likely just because their parents served them boiled. When roasted or steamed, as in this recipe, they're actually delicious.

COOKING TIME: 15 MINUTES | SERVINGS: 2

Ingredients:

- 16 oz. Brussels sprouts
- ½ cup unsweetened dry cranberries
- ½ cup crumbled goat or feta cheese
- 8 oz. cooked quinoa
- 2 tbsp. balsamic salad dressing

Directions:

1. Place the Brussels sprouts in a microwave-safe ceramic bowl, cover with pierced clingfilm, and microwave for 3 minutes until fork-tender. Slice the sprouts into quarters lengthwise and add in the cranberries and cheese.

2. Microwave the quinoa to re-heat. Toss all the ingredients with the salad dressing to coat and serve.

SALADS & SIDE DISHES

ITALIAN GREEN BEANS

A little acidity from the tomato, along with some flavoring, is all string beans need to reach their full potential.

COOKING TIME: 25 MINUTES | SERVINGS: 8

INGREDIENTS:

- 1½ lbs. string beans
- 1 tbsp. Extra-virgin olive oil
- 1 tsp. Italian herb mix
- 2 cups cherry tomatoes
- ½ cup grated Parmesan cheese

DIRECTIONS:

1. Set oven to 425 °F (220 °C) and leave to heat while you prepare your ingredients.

2. Grease a roasting pan with cooking spray or olive oil. Trim the ends off the beans and cut them in half. Slice the tomatoes in half.

3. Whisk the olive oil, Italian herbs, and salt and pepper to taste into a dressing. Stir the dressing into the beans to coat before adding the beans to a roasting pan.

4. Bake for 10 minutes, stirring halfway through.

5. Add the cherry tomatoes and return to the oven for approximately 5 more minutes.

6. Garnish with the cheese to serve.

DESSERTS

DESSERTS

IMITATION HAZELNUT PIE

Hazelnuts are kind of expensive and pies are usually difficult to bake. But... you could just use Nutella and sidestep both problems!

COOKING TIME: 10 MINUTES | SERVINGS: 8

Ingredients:

- 8 oz. tub cream cheese
- 1 cup powdered sugar
- 1¼ cups Nutella
- 8 oz. carton frozen whipped dessert topping, thawed in fridge
- 1x 9" baked chocolate pie crust

Directions:

1. Use an electric beater to whisk together the cream cheese, sugar, and 1 cup Nutella until creamy. Then, gently fold in the dessert topping.

2. Spoon the filling into the pie crust in an even layer.

3. Place the rest of the Nutella into a cup, microwave for 20 seconds to melt, and drip over the filling in an attractive pattern.

4. Chill in the fridge overnight before serving (Note: the pie needs a minimum of 4 hours in the fridge to set properly).

DESSERTS

OVEN-BAKED S'MORES

There's little camping in winter, but you can always recreate the s'more taste for snacking in front of the TV.

COOKING TIME: 25 MINUTES | SERVINGS: 8

INGREDIENTS:

- 8 oz. tube crescent roll dough
- ¼ cup Nutella spread
- 1¼ cornflakes
- 2 tbsp. chocolate chips
- 2/3 cup miniature marshmallows

DIRECTIONS:

1. Pre-heat oven to 375 °F (190 °C). Line a baking sheet with parchment paper.

2. Take the dough out of the packaging and separate into 8 triangular pieces.

3. Spoon a small dollop of Nutella onto the wide end of each pastry triangle. Top with the crushed cornflakes, chocolate chips, and marshmallows.

4. Roll up the pastry portions into tubes from the chocolate end. Place on the baking sheet with the tip of the seam at the bottom. Bend into semicircles.

5. Bake for approximately 10 minutes, or until the pastry is crisp and golden.

6. Microwave the remaining Nutella (approx. 1 tbsp.) until liquid. Drizzle over the rolls.

DESSERTS

VANILLA-AND-FRUIT KOLACHES

These Central European pastries can contain either sweet or savory fillings and come in many shapes. This version simplifies making the dough.

COOKING TIME: 1½ HOUR | SERVINGS: 10 DOZEN

INGREDIENTS:

- 2 cups butter, at room temperature
- 1 pint vanilla ice cream, not too cold
- 4 cups all-purpose flour
- 2 tbsp. sugar
- 24 oz. cans apricot, cherry, almond, or raspberry cake and pastry filling

DIRECTIONS:

1. Set oven to 350 °F (175 °C) and let it heat up while you prepare your ingredients. Line two baking trays with parchment paper.

2. Use an electric beater to whisk the ice cream and butter together. Stir in the flour and sugar.

3. Separate the dough into 4 balls and place in the fridge for 2 hours.

4. Sprinkle additional flour onto a clean, dry countertop. Working with one ball of dough at a time, roll the dough into a square of about 11" a side before slicing into 2" squares.

5. Lay one tsp. filling in the center of each square. Fold into triangles and crimp the sides closed.

6. Arrange the dough triangles on the baking trays, with 2" of space between each triangle. Bake for approximately 12 minutes, or until the pastries are slightly browned.

7. Allow the pastries to stand in the cooling oven for 1 minute before transferring to a cooling rack. Sprinkle with powdered sugar.

DESSERTS

WHITE CHOCOLATE RICE KRISPIES TREATS

Since there's little cooking and no baking involved in preparing these, you may want to enlist your kids' help and make a glorious mess in the kitchen.

COOKING TIME: 15 MINUTES | SERVINGS: 3 DOZEN

Ingredients:

- 4 cups mini marshmallows
- 8 oz. white chocolate chips
- ¼ cup butter
- 6 cups Rice Krispies-type cereal

Directions:

1. Cut the butter into cubes and add it to a crockpot or bain-marie, along with the chocolate chips and marshmallows.

2. Melt on low heat. When done, stir in the Rice Krispies until thoroughly mixed.

3. Scrape the mixture into a baking pan greased with additional butter. Gently compact the mixture into an even layer. Once set, cut into bars or squares.

DESSERTS

EASY BLUEBERRY COBBLER

Blueberries are in season from late spring to early fall, but you can substitute almost any fresh fruit you have on hand.

COOKING TIME: 50 MINUTES | SERVINGS: 9

INGREDIENTS:

- 1 egg
- ½ cup canola oil
- ¾ cup whole milk
- 15 oz. box cornbread mix
- 1 cup fresh blueberries
- Vanilla ice cream or cream, optional

DIRECTIONS:

1. Pre-heat oven to 350 °F (180 °C). Grease a small ceramic casserole pan.

2. Whisk together the oil, milk, egg, and sugar to taste. Combine this mixture with the cornbread mix and stir until just evenly moist.

3. Spoon the dough into the pan in an even layer. Top with blueberries.

4. Bake for 35 minutes.

5. Serve with vanilla ice cream or cream if desired.

DESSERTS

VANILLA CAKE WITH COOKIE PIECES

A little bit of added texture goes a long way in livening up an everyday cake.

COOKING TIME: 50 MINUTES | SERVINGS: 9

Ingredients:

- 5 oz. butter
- 2 eggs
- 2 cups whole milk
- 16 oz. box vanilla cake mix
- 10 Joe-Joe's cookies or Oreos

Directions:

1. Pre-heat oven to 350°F (180°C). Coat a small, high-sided baking tray with cooking spray.

2. Cut the butter into cubes and place it in a small bowl. Microwave until melted.

3. Beat the butter, milk, and eggs until well combined.

4. Add in a little of the cake mixture, mix, and repeat until you've used all of the cake mix. The batter should be smooth and without any lumps.

5. Place the cookies in a plastic bag and mash into rough crumbs. Stir into the batter.

6. Bake for 35 minutes, or until a toothpick inserted into the center comes out dry.

7. Allow the cake to cool completely before coating with frosting, if so desired.

DESSERTS

ALMOND BISCOTTIS

Not only is almond flour delicious in its own right, but it's gluten-free, more nutritious than wheat, and lends itself well to crispy pastries.

COOKING TIME: 45 MINUTES | SERVINGS: 15

INGREDIENTS:

- 2 egg whites
- ½ cup honey or maple syrup
- 2¼ cups almond flour (not almond meal)
- ¾ tsp. almond or vanilla essence
- 1 cup sliced almonds, finely chopped

DIRECTIONS:

1. Pre-heat oven to 325 °F (160 °C). Line a baking sheet with wax paper.

2. Whisk 1 egg white with the maple syrup and a pinch of salt until airy. Drip in the almond or vanilla essence and whisk just enough to mix.

3. Gradually fold the almond flour into the beaten egg white. Once done, put aside for a quarter of an hour while the flour absorbs the moisture.

4. Beat the second egg white until fluffy in a separate bowl.

5. Wet your hands and a large spoon. Use both to form the batter into balls. (Note: the very sticky batter won't adhere to wet surfaces).

6. Coat the balls with the second egg white, then dip it into the chopped almonds.

7. Arrange the balls on the baking sheet with at least 1" space between each.

8. Bake for 30-35 minutes until slightly browned. Transfer to a wire rack to cool.

DESSERTS

SEASONAL BERRY BLANC MANGE

Here's proof that anyone can whip up an incredibly elegant-looking dessert.

COOKING TIME: 35 MINUTES | SERVINGS: 4

Ingredients:

- 1¼ cup fresh berries (blackberries, blueberries, strawberries, or raspberries)
- 1¼ tsp. gelatin powder
- 8¾ oz. can coconut cream
- 3 tbsp. honey or maple syrup
- ½ tsp. lemon juice

Directions:

1. Simmer the berries in a small saucepan for 15-20 minutes.

2. Mix the gelatin with 1¼ tbsp. water and set aside while it absorbs the moisture.

3. Whisk the coconut cream, berry mixture, and honey or syrup thoroughly until silky in texture.

4. Strain the mixture through a fine sieve to catch the seeds and then return to the saucepan. Heat, add the gelatin, and stir until mixed well. Remove the mixture from the heat and stir in the lemon juice.

5. Transfer the mixture into small bowls lined with plastic wrap and leave to cool. Once at room temperature, move to the fridge and let them firm up for at least 2 hours.

6. To serve, invert the molds onto small plates and garnish with chocolate sprinkles, mint leaves, or whatever you prefer.

DESSERTS

BAKLAVA MADE EASY

Following the traditional method is for professional chefs and people with too much time on their hands. Our way is much quicker.

COOKING TIME: 60 MINUTES | SERVINGS: 24

INGREDIENTS:

- 1 lb. walnuts, almonds, hazelnuts, or cashews
- 1½ tsp. ground cinnamon
- 16 oz. package frozen filo dough, thawed slowly in the refrigerator
- 1 cup butter
- 1 cup honey

DIRECTIONS:

1. Pre-heat oven to 350 °F (175 °C). Line a baking sheet with parchment paper.

2. If whole, chop the nuts by pulsing in a blender or food processor. Mix with the cinnamon.

3. Cut the butter into cubes and melt using the microwave.

4. Spread out the dough and loosely separate the individual sheets. Place two sheets on the baking sheet and, using a kitchen brush, baste the top with melted butter. Perform the same procedure with six more individual sheets. (Note: lay a damp kitchen cloth over the unused dough to keep it moist and pliable while you work.)

5. Top the last sheet with ½ a cup chopped nuts and 2 tbsp. honey. Layer over another two pastry sheets, add more nuts and honey – do this six times, or until you run out of chopped nuts.

6. Slice part of the way through the assembled baklava to separate two dozen portions. Bake for approximately 25 minutes, or until the top is browned and crunchy. Transfer to a wire rack to cool.

DESSERTS

TOASTED ANGEL FOOD CAKE

Only a little effort is needed to completely transform a store-bought dessert staple.

COOKING TIME: 15 MINUTES | SERVINGS: 8

INGREDIENTS:

- 9 oz. fresh strawberries
- 2 tsp. granulated sugar
- 3 tbsp. butter
- 2 tbsp. balsamic vinegar
- 8 oz. prepared angel food cake

DIRECTIONS:

1. Slice the strawberries and mix with the sugar in a large bowl.

2. Melt the butter in the microwave. Whisk together with the balsamic.

3. Slice the cake into 8 portions and then brush the vinegar mixture onto the cut surfaces.

4. Grill or broil the cake over medium heat until a crispy crust forms (approx. 1-2 minutes per side).

5. Serve topped with strawberries. Add vanilla ice cream and fruit syrup if you like.

DESSERTS

NUTTY CHOCOLATE SQUARES

Made from ingredients you're likely to have in your pantry, these squares are perfect to appease an itchy sweet tooth without having to run to the store.

PREP TIME: 20 MINUTES | SERVINGS: 24

INGREDIENTS:

- ¾ cup crushed cornflakes
- ½ cup butter
- 2 cups powdered sugar
- ½ cup chunky peanut butter
- 1 cup chocolate chips

DIRECTIONS:

1. Melt the butter in the microwave and stir into the cornflake crumbs. Combine this with the sugar and peanut butter.

2. Spread an even layer in an 8"-square dish. Melt the chocolate chips in the microwave – stir until no lumps remain – and drizzle over the mixture in the pan.

3. Place in the fridge for half an hour before slicing into two dozen squares. Return to the fridge to set completely (approx. another half an hour). Store chilled.

Tip: Chocolate chips vary hugely in quality. When in doubt, pick the more expensive kind.

DESSERTS

HOMEMADE CHOCOLATE TRUFFLES

This recipe is way cheaper to make than purchasing the fancy store-bought candy – and these little delights easily hold their own against most brands.

PREP TIME: 15 MINUTES | SERVINGS: 30

INGREDIENTS:

- 12 oz. dark chocolate chips
- ¾ cup heavy cream
- 1 tsp. orange or lemon essence
- 1/3 cup sugar

DIRECTIONS:

1. Heat the chocolate chips in microwave, stirring occasionally. Once melted, add in the cream, a little at a time. Stir constantly until well combined. Add in the citrus essence and stir.

2. Cool to room temperature, stirring from time to time to keep mixture consistent. When relatively stiff, use two spoons to form the mixture into balls ¾" across (Note: you may have to put the balls in the fridge for a few minutes to harden).

3. Place sugar in a saucer or shallow bowl and coat the truffles by dabbing them into the sugar.

DESSERTS

PEAR PIE

The kind of sugar found in fruit (and therefore juice) tastes a lot sweeter than ordinary granulated sugar. This means that this pie will satisfy your sweet tooth even though it's low in calories.

COOKING TIME: 45 MINUTES | SERVINGS: 8

INGREDIENTS:

- 1 sheet refrigerated pie crust
- 4 fresh pears (anjou or bartlett varieties are best)
- 1/3 cup dried cranberries
- 1/3 cup 100% apple juice concentrate
- 1 tsp. apple pie spice mix

DIRECTIONS:

1. Pre-heat oven to 375 °F (190 °C).

2. Peel and slice the pears.

3. Mold the pie crust into a 9" tart pan with a separate base. Poke holes in the bottom using a fork and trim off the excess dough.

4. Place a large saucepan on medium heat and cook the apple juice concentrate, spice mix, pears, and cranberries until a fork enters the pears easily.

5. Add the filling to the crust. Bake for approximately 35 minutes, or until the crust has a nice color. Transfer to a wire rack to cool.

Made in the USA
Coppell, TX
30 November 2022